Ferdinand Hand, Walter Edward Lawson

Aesthetics of Musical Art

Or, the beautiful in music. Second Edition

Ferdinand Hand, Walter Edward Lawson

Aesthetics of Musical Art
Or, the beautiful in music. Second Edition

ISBN/EAN: 9783337084462

Printed in Europe, USA, Canada, Australia, Japan

Cover: Foto ©Thomas Meinert / pixelio.de

More available books at **www.hansebooks.com**

ÆSTHETICS

OF

MUSICAL ART;

OR,

THE BEAUTIFUL IN MUSIC.

BY

DR. FERDINAND HAND.

TRANSLATED FROM THE GERMAN
BY
WALTER E. LAWSON,
MUS. BAC. CANTAB., ETC.

BOOK THE FIRST.

SECOND EDITION.

LONDON:
WILLIAM REEVES, 185, FLEET STREET.
(Office of "Reeves' Musical Directory" and "The Musical Standard.")

1880.

LONDON: BOWDEN, HUDSON AND CO., PRINTERS,
23, RED LION STREET, HOLBORN.

CONTENTS.

	PAGE
Translator's Preface	vii
Preface	xi
Introduction	1
Book the First.—Of the Nature of Music . .	17
Chap. I.—Of the music of Nature in general . .	19
Of Tone	25
Rhythm	33
The relation of tones in acuteness and gravity	45
The music of Nature beyond the human sphere	48
Chap. II.—Of the music of mankind . .	61
Music the product of free self-activity of the mind	62
Music the immediate representation of the activity of the feelings	96

CHAPTER II.—*continued.*

Music the product of the spirituality and of
    the totality of the powers of the mind . 127
Melody 132
Harmony 149
Free play in tone-pictures 177
Modification of expression . . 182
Subordination to the idea of Beauty . . 187

TRANSLATOR'S PREFACE.

Æsthetics is the name originally given to the philosophical theory of the Beautiful by the German philosopher Baumgarten, who derived it from the Greek word *aisthetikos*, signifying, I begin to perceive, or I am sensible. That this term is quite inadequate to express the nature, or object of the science, is obvious, although, from an entirely different point of view, it may not seem ill-chosen, seeing that even at the present day, we are but *becoming* sensible of beauty as a given property of objects.

Æsthetics has not long ranked as a separate science, but since Baumgarten's attempt at an exposition (*Æsthetik*, Frankfort, 1750), numerous works of the kind have appeared in

Germany. It must be admitted that the subject is peculiarly congenial to the German intellect, and that the German language is vastly rich in words suited to the expression of this and kindred subjects. The paucity (absence?) of works of this nature in our own tongue is remarkable, and is perhaps only to be accounted for on the supposition that the English, as a nation, are more practical, and less speculative, than their Teutonic brethren.

The present work is, I believe, generally regarded as being the best amongst those which treat of Æsthetics with exclusive reference to musical art, and we may naturally feel surprised that, as such, it should be the production of an amateur. Yet it is so. Dr. Ferdinand Gotthelf Hand, privy councillor, and professor of Greek literature, was born at Plauen, in Saxon Voigtland, on the 15th February, 1780. He studied philology at the University of Leipzig, and proceeded to his degree in 1809. In 1817 he was nominated professor at the University of Jena, and not only attained to repute in the pursuit of his avocation, but also as the director of the Academy Concerts held in that town. He died in Jena on the 14th March, 1851.

Since the publication of Dr. Hand's treatise, but few works on the Æsthetics of Music have been given to the world, notwithstanding the fact that the, now, well-sifted critical disquisitions into the peculiarities and artistic value of the poetic compositions of Schumann, Chopin, Sterndale Bennett, &c., have rendered a further development of the science possible and even necessary, at the same time securing to us, by virtue of the reaction, a deeper insight into the works of the classical period of Beethoven and Mozart. There is ample scope for a further treatment of the subject from a more modern point of view, which would, doubtless, necessitate a reconstruction of the old system.

This work now passes out of my hands into the hands of those who are more competent than I to judge of its merits and demerits. Such being the case, I would merely ask that those persons who are indebted to me for its reproduction under the altered circumstances of language, will not be too severe in their criticisms of my modest effort, seeing that I was thrown entirely upon my own resources for an intelligible English terminology, having no native work to guide me; I would further remind them that a translation, even when more conscientiously performed than that now before the reader, must ever fall short of the original; and lastly, I trust that no one will charge me with assuming too much when I say that, with the exception of certain lectures delivered at South Kensington by Mr. Ernst Pauer, the present attempt is the first that has been made to popularize the science of Æsthetics in this country. Weak as I now feel my endeavours at a translation to have been, and vividly conscious of the pithy remark of a certain poet, I would still beg the indulgent reader to place my good intentions in the balance with all crudities of composition.

WALTER E. LAWSON.

BRIXTON.

PREFACE.

HAD a general concurrence enforced the opinion advanced by Nägeli to the effect that it is hardly permissible to the Dilettante to speak on matters appertaining to musical art, I should have laid this attempt before my readers with a greater show of diffidence than I do under the existing circumstances. As it is, I can meet the reproof with the conviction that, should the undertaking fail in my unskilful hands, the blame will attach to the artists by profession, who, being more directly concerned, should have taken up the subject, and not have tacitly committed it to the hands of an Amateur.

Our literature does not as yet include a work

upon Musical Æsthetics, and the information upon the subject which is to be gleaned from treatises on General Æsthetics is not sufficient. The necessity for such a work became daily more manifest, for in the periodicals, works were judged from an æsthetical point of view, and were referred to principles which, if existing, were, at all events, nowhere clearly explained. The readers of these periodicals will agree with me, that a thorough confusion of language prevails in them, consequent upon the many different views taken of the matter; while, not seldom, a vague manner of expression, in which a leading principle was wanting, was the cause of a failure in the result.

This state of things called loudly for redress, and promises of an Æsthetics of Music came from many quarters, but none of them were fulfilled. After a few attempts at a representation on a scientific basis, a fundamental idea would at length prevail, and the gain to artistic productiveness would not be wanting. An earnest commencement must now be made.

No one can tell me so emphatically as I myself, of the weaknesses under which this work labours—its foundation does not appear sufficiently comprehensive, the references to examples should be more abundant, as a composition it lacks fluency and elegance; but should anyone say that this book contains much that is already known or recognised as uncontrovertible truth, it can hardly be construed into a reproach, seeing that it was simply intended to collect that which is already generally received, and reconstruct it upon a more solid foundation. Every particular shall be systematically arranged.

There is yet one thing that I am candid enough to admit, it is, that that which is here laid before the reader, without arrogance and destitute of polemical tendencies, is a product of the warmest and purest love for the art. As such, may it meet with a friendly reception, and be the means of inducing others, more intelligent, soon to supply a better.

The order which I have adhered to throughout the investigation is explained in the Introduction. The book itself I wish to be regarded as an educational work, that no one may expect to find in it a means of delightfully amusing himself, but, rather, be induced thereby to think more deeply, and to aim at the further development of the hints which it contains.

The second part, which will contain the Æsthetical Rules of Composition, will follow the present volume as quickly as the leisure time at my disposal will admit.

F. HAND.

JENA, 12*th August*, 1837.

INTRODUCTION.

§ I.

TO speak of music, and to judge musical works according to a certain fixed standard of legality, is in many respects difficult, and where the understanding is not quite clear, far more hazardous than the majority of those who allow themselves freedom in this respect are wont to imagine. The subject regarded in itself, does not fall within the province of the understanding and the ideas, and is sometimes difficult to convey by means of words; rather must it be drawn within the province of the imagination, and gained therefrom by abstraction.

Vain would be the attempt to demonstrate to a man of understanding only, a property which requires an ear and a heart for its thorough comprehension. The supposition that Æsthetics consists of formal ideas, sometimes leads to an unsuccessful attempt to teach that which can alone be grasped by the whole Soul.

On the other hand, every person draws a standard of judgment from the sphere of his individual feelings, and thus forms an opinion in accordance with the principle, that within the province of the feelings, no call is made for general arbitration. In the endeavour to arrive at some rule the majority of writers are apt to lose themselves in unclear thoughts, buried beneath the empty forms and inaccurate definitions of a fantastic language, and, for all the number of words used and their florid character, nothing is propounded, or at least nothing is proved.

Indeed, the way in which a judgment of a musical work is formed, itself increases the difficulty. The painting and the statue are visible to the eye, and can be observed with quietude and with a fixed regard; but a work of musical art passes over, and scarcely leaves us a moment for thought. A simple reading of the notes, although often considered sufficient by the art critic, can never answer the purpose of an immediate perception of living tone.

Nevertheless, these difficulties and the danger of misconception, must not render us fearful of making an attempt. We should also have to preserve a silence on such themes as Religion and Love, and the Beautiful in general, were it denied us to search thoughtfully into the innermost and most secret recesses of the Soul for the law by which the creative power of genius originates works of art. And by whom, in the ordinary paths of life, has not the want of an explanation of the nature and value of art-works been felt, more particularly from a desire to become clear as to what musical Beauty is, and how it operates, what may constitute the boundaries of this art province, and in what forms the musical art creates and asserts itself.

The purpose of the elucidation is only to be attained under a twofold condition.

In the first place let it be taken for granted that in the vast region of the Soul's activity, not everything comes home to the ideas, and not everything receives confirmation from the deductions of the understanding, but requires, from a vivifying belief, a something final and undemonstrable, which may be recognised and grasped as an actuality.

One such thing is the recognition of Truth, another the immediate perception of the Beautiful, inasmuch as these phenomena of existence contain a finality, rising beyond the region of the ideas, which is given to the belief in an Infinity, and of which we, in our feelings, become sensible. Here the hint must suffice.

The second condition which helps to render an understanding possible, lies in the participation in the establishment of a fundamental principle. Until all are agreed as to the general nature of music, conflicting opinions will preclude the possibility of a true and sufficiently comprehensive assessment of the Beautiful in music, nor will any person who has not made clear to himself such fundamental principle, be in a position to form a correct estimate of, or even to fully comprehend, a single work of art.

Nowhere do we find, so daily experience teaches us, such undigested observations, and empty utterances, often hidden beneath a fantastic and brilliant language, as in matters belonging to musical art. The majority pretend to feel that which cannot possibly be felt, and from poverty of clear ideas, make use of representations and comparisons to explain that which they assume to be unutterable, without in the slightest degree clearing up the subject.

No doubt we must allow that everyone has a right to speak on human affairs, if it be done without arrogance; and if the æsthetical criticism of musical works falls principally within that circle distinguished by the name of Dilettante, and musicians by profession are not seldom disdainfully overlooked, on the other hand it may be observed that but few artists are competent with respect to art-philosophy, or able to enlighten us on matters of canon.

These considerations may serve to enlarge our sphere of observation.

§ II.

IN this investigation we must not neglect to take into consideration the music prior to and distinct from the art-work. The Primitive and the Universal we must regard as a basis, resolve it into its elements, and seek to discover the one nature which it exhibits under all forms. Intellectual life in its relation to the sensuous phenomenon of tone must be clearly explained, and the secret of the soul's innermost existence receive an interpretation; the province of art, to which Beauty first attaches itself, must be brought within more definite boundaries, and its laws explained with sufficient validity.

In the accomplishment of this task the question naturally arises whether our enquiries shall be directed to the music which sounds and is sung, or to that which is appreciable and is heard; whether the object of music consists in its being expressed or sung, or whether it exists simply to delight when listened to. Is the performance of a musical work only a copy of the art-work or the art-work itself? Or are musical works, without performance, like badly hung paintings? Is, to one who plays or sings in the absence of other listeners than himself, his own perception by hearing, or the expression of his individual feelings, the principal matter? If these questions remain unanswered misunderstandings can but result.

In former times Athanasius Kircher, and at a more recent period Nägeli, wrote concerning music which is heard, which produces effect. Others, on the contrary, have addressed themselves solely to that which is composed, to the product of the mind. If an art-work exists that it may be grasped by the ideas, and may please, or that it may convey to the mind an ideal satisfaction, then music may be said to strive, in the first degree, after utterance, and to desire to express in song and play that which moves the heart.

In it we observe the Subjective and Objective united, inasmuch as the performance of an unknown composition is but a reproduction of the original, and the person who performs regards as his own the feelings which he has but adopted, while he who listens feels the same excited within him.

§ III.

THE æsthetical treatment of music is, in all cases where a systematic foundation, and the derivation of art rules are concerned, rendered difficult by the absence of previous efforts. From a remote period, the system of general æsthetics has been cautiously added to, and securely based, so that for every successive investigation a rich store of information was available; the special Poetik found its elaborators; music, alone, shared with painting the lot to be kept back, to the great detriment of the subject in general. If æstheticians had carried their arguments into the province of musical art, they would have become aware of the unsatisfactory nature of many of their theorems.

Long since had music developed into an art, and had contained the Beautiful, but for all that it remained but an object of enjoyment or veneration, without being drawn within the sphere of æsthetical observation. The philosophers despised it, or at least did not trouble to ask themselves whether a science of musical art were also possible. Scientists busied themselves only with the technical and mathematical contents. Until the development of a science of the Beautiful, and of the Fine-arts, by Germans, a foundation was wanting. In the musical works which have been handed down to us from ancient times, the æsthetical always forms the weakest part.

To what extent Pythagoras was acquainted, in music, with the law of well ordered ratios, and the mathematical basis, pointed out its parallel in the laws of moral life, and practically studied the educational influence of the art, is only known to us in a general way. Plato, from a more elevated point of view, recognised in music the expression of the inner life, as a representation of the various conditions of the mind, and regarded the idea of the Beautiful as its foundation, which—as moral beauty combined with that which is good—emanates from God, and therefore leads to unison with God.

He raised the purpose of music beyond that of mere sensuous enjoyment, and censured those who valued it only in proportion to the amount of amusement which it provided for them. Inasmuch as he condemned, as being too artificial, the use of instruments independently of poetry, he doubtless wished to withdraw music from the part which it took in the mere gratification of the senses, to a higher world of thought, for he also saw in it a fountain of the purest harmony of life, and a revelation of the Divine idea. Herewith a notion of the intellectual character of music was gained, and of the great scope which was offered for developing the unity of the idea of the Beautiful and Good.

Aristotle did not differ from these views to any material extent. He, also, ascribed to music an intellectual and divine character; beheld in it a free art, which neither served a useful purpose nor as a pastime; and recognised its influence in the noble occupation of the mind, and as a means of moral education. Poetics alone developed his æsthetical views more thoroughly.

To the Pythagoreans, who were called Canonici, and their mathematical theory, Aristoxenus opposed himself with the assertion, that in musical matters not only the understanding but also the ear judges, and thus led up to the question, What part do understanding, perception, and feeling simultaneously take in music? But he failed to arrive at any definite results.

Among the remaining writers on musical subjects, who for the most part treated only of the tonal system, Claudius Ptolomæus can alone be mentioned as having, at a later date, without reference to any other authority secured the science of Harmony on a firmer basis, and while tracing the origin of music to the feelings, expounded clearer views with regard to key characteristic.

However valuable may be the acute views and reflections of the ancient writers upon the significance of music, and its influence upon life, still a general fundamental view, and a theory, were not to be thought of while music was but regarded as a handmaid of Poesy. Art here also was in advance of theory. This we learn from the History of Music in the Christian era, which also makes known to us the fact that the theoretical matter treated of up to that time, was confined to the grammar, or the mathematical-technical part of the art,—to Thorough-bass and the Art of Composition. Concerning what pleases us in tones, and how it pleases, but few troubled themselves. Still music was not regarded as a fine art, in which a deeper penetration into the nature of the Beautiful was taken for granted; this only became possible as the whole province of the psychological was defined and arranged.

To the school of the philosophers Wolf and Baumgarten belongs the credit of having again drawn the Beautiful into the province of philosophical discussion, and of having set up, side by side with Logic, and Ethics, an Æsthetic, as science of the Beautiful and of the Fine Arts. The Beautiful, however, was regarded as equivalent to the Perfect, and the conditions under which anything pleases, were derived from the idea of Perfection; on the other hand, the recognition of the Beautiful as sensuous, was held to be a confused and indistinct view of the matter. The other arts, however, soon found their æsthetical elaborators: Painting in Hagedorn and Mengs, Sculpture in Winkelmann, and Poetry in Lessing. Music alone remained disregarded, and no one saw in it more than "the representation of passionate emotions." The Beautiful was either left wholly unnoticed, or but casually mentioned. And thus it remained, until Kant, by tracing the limits of the spheres of the soul's activity, became the founder of an art-philosophy. Music he regarded indeed as but a pleasing play of the emotions excited from without, but he failed to make clear to himself whether a mere sensuous impression, or the effect of a discernment, of form prevailed in that play.

No contents make a claim upon our consideration, where the tones contain in themselves both Means and End, and only aim at exciting the sensuous perceptions. As Kant did not allow music to be the language of the emotions, and a means of awakening æsthetical ideas, all that was left to him, to associate with a fertility of thought, was the mathematical form made use of in amalgamating the sensations; and inasmuch as with regard to charm and the power of animating the feelings, he ranked music below poetry, so he assigned to it, from an intellectual point of view, the lowest position amongst the arts, seeing that it merely affects the sensations.

The later investigations of the Idealists and Natural Philosophers led to an important change, inasmuch as through them an art-science resulted, in which the arts were arranged as members of a great Whole. Some insisted upon the recognition of a higher significance in music, and claimed for it a participation in an ideal Beauty; others associated Nature, and the Mind, and pointed out the unity which exists between them, and explained the relation which Art bears to Nature, all of which had a considerable influence upon the special Æsthetics. Still no one attempted a work upon the Æsthetics of musical art. That which has been given out under this title in Schubert's papers contains much valuable matter; that which Wilhelmj Müller (Leipzig, 1830) has termed musical æsthetics, is far removed from scientific investigation. Greatly to be esteemed are Seidel's contributions to *Charinomos*, and those of certain writers to the *Musikalische Zeitung* and *Cäcilia*. Much that is acute and excellent is to be found scattered through other æsthetical papers.

§ IV.

THE scientific endeavours to secure a foundation for the views regarding the Beautiful and Art, never failed to exert an influence upon art-culture, though it would be difficult to show how the theories of the schools thus became effective. Art strikes its own path, preceding theory; but in cases where the doctrines of philosophy pass into, and become fundamental ideas of life, their influence upon art products can be shown. This is confirmed by the *History of Music*, and proves the value of æsthetical observation in relation to the progressive development of art. Leibnitz guided by his own philosophical views of things, could but complain of the too artificial character of the music of his time. Richardson's Romances were expressive of the principles of English moralising æsthetics, Schiller's Tragedies are the fruit of an idealistic soil; and the principles maintained by Rousseau, by which music has only to please the ear, have asserted themselves throughout a lengthened period. On the other hand, the great compositions in the strict and earnest style of Handel and Bach, could only have been the produce of a time when there was neither necessity for a soft sentimentality, excited by fictitious affections, nor for art, originating in a fantastic philosophy of life, but rather, when the feelings bore in themselves a strong belief in religion, and the understanding maintained the balance of healthy reflection. Mozart, seizing directly upon the Beautiful, strove after contents and perspicuity. Beethoven was an Idealist, and having the power to lend an ideal beauty to the most minute and seemingly unimportant matter, strove after universal harmonies.

Even with regard to the value of music, and of its kinds, opinions have, from a remote period, been at variance. Some will only recognise music when it is associated with poetry, and declare, with Hegel, that instrumental music is empty and incomprehensible; others approve only of the ancient and strict church style; and close the list of original writers with Handel and Bach. Not even where the Nature of music is called into question, have they been able to avoid the dangers of extremes; and one altogether denies to it intellectual import, another sees in it the language of an earthly felicity. In more recent times, the disputants have divided themselves into two parties, of which the one sees in music only a play of well sounding tones, and even goes so far as to assert that the more empty it is, the better it fulfils its purpose; the other bases all upon a predominating significance. The former do not consider that a work of fine-art in which an idea is invariably present, is quite out of the question where tones are simply sported with; the latter overlook the fact, that Beauty can of itself satisfy, without borrowing a prop from the province of the understanding and reflection. Where such differences exist, nought but an enlightened rudimentary idea of the nature of music, and of the Beautiful in musical art, can be the means of securing a firm judgment, and of making its theoretical influence felt. On many points all are agreed, and a mutual explanation alone is necessary, while even where opinions are divided, the truth is usually present, although it may be somewhat obscured. This may serve us for consolation and comfort.

§ V.

ÆSTHETICS is the name given to the Science of the Beautiful, or to the contemplative existence governed by the idea of the Beautiful, in contradistinction to the Sciences of the True and Good, or Logic, Metaphysics and Ethics. Its general foundation and position in the province of philosophical discipline, we may assume to be explained elsewhere, and we need be under no concern because the name does not precisely express its purport, seeing that it can neither be exchanged for that of Science of the Taste, nor, without still greater ambiguity, for Science of Art.

If the purpose of general æsthetics be to determine the nature of the Beautiful, and to consider its forms theoretically, to describe the faculties of the mind called into activity by the Beautiful, and to explain the position which it occupies with regard to life; and if it proceed in the second degree to consider the laws of the representation of the Beautiful in Art; then a special æsthetics should treat of the same subjects with reference to a particular sphere of art. Therefore we possess the Æsthetics of musical art, as of the plastic arts and poetry, according as the Beautiful is expressed in tones, or forms, or in thought-pictures and words; and explanation shall be given as to what constitutes the pleasing and the ideal in tones, and how the musical artist imparts to his works an æsthetical contents.

§ VI.

THE Science of tones may be divided into three branches, the physical, the mathematical and the æsthetical. The physical nature of tones, how they are produced and become perceptible, is taught by Acoustics. The Canonic treats of the value and mutual relation of tones; and their combinations, and, in the science of composition, gives the rules for their treatment.

The science of Æsthetics regards the fine-art music as an object of investigation, in order to ascertan how the Beautiful is made apparent in works of this art, and what it is that makes a musical product a work of art. Far removed from it is formal technic, which in a work of musical instruction, remains the subject of treatment only as far as it may be unassociated with a higher intellectual significance; and even that which is formal in respect of Melody and Harmony, and constitutes the scientific part of composition, does not wholly come under consideration. But inasmuch as it makes the Intellectual a subject of investigation, and treats of the Beautiful in musical works, it cannot proceed securely, until an understanding is arrived at as to what music may represent, and how such representation is made. Consequently we may not forego to speak of the Nature of Music generally, or to regard the whole tone-world, even as it is, without the perfect impress of Beauty; for we should but erroneously ascribe to tone itself, a Beauty which does not primarily dwell within it. If we may allow ourselves the definition, such a science is a Philosophy of Music.

§ VII.

IN the following investigation we shall endeavour to complete, in four books, the tasks here briefly mentioned. The first of these books will treat of the Nature of music; the second of the Beautiful in musical art; the third of the laws of musical art works in general; the fourth of the rules relating to individual musical works. We shall commence by fixing the boundary line which divides the province of Nature from that of Art, and by following the æsthetical element in its separation from the natural material, and in its gradual development to perfect Beauty. Arrived at the Art-work we shall then have to seek out the universal art rules for the invention of a musical work, and to explain the peculiarities and legality of the various kinds of art forms hitherto invented and made use of.

BOOK THE FIRST.

OF THE NATURE OF MUSIC.

IN a certain sense, as the following investigation will show, music falls to the lot of mankind only, who regards it from the province of intellectual life, wherein the word and the idea have a narrow signification and only become perfectly valid when used in reference to art. In a broader and more universal sense, music —inclusive even of the Beautiful which pervades it— belongs to the whole of Nature, and to every being possessing intelligence. The Beautiful does not confine itself within the limits of human art, but is not less apparent in the creations of Nature, and indeed earlier than and before all art, although it perhaps exists for mankind alone. Therefore our first observations must be directed to the Music of Nature in general. It forms the foundation of all that which is to follow, and must be made to take in the full import of the presence of an intelligent, and, in many different grades, efficient existence.

This investigation shall not proceed from a definition which could only pass current as the explanation of a term, but shall rather, by the progressive discussion of particulars, secure such a grasp of the whole subject that a general principle must of itself result.

CHAPTER I.

OF THE MUSIC OF NATURE IN GENERAL.

§ I.

WHEREVER life is found, it appears, however various the spheres of its existence may be, as *Motion*. Active forces make themselves known, for a rigid restraint gives place to free movement, the fetters of an outer necessity are broken, and Rest is converted into Motion. All life has motion. The phenomenon of life presupposes—and is thus far independent of outer conditions—an inner power, which asserts itself in the same, and of itself unknown, thus becomes recognisable. Therefore wherever in Nature we perceive life, it is always a Manifestation, the result of an inner force, a motion derived from within.

The nature of this phenomenon is twofold. In the first case it is observable in the works of Nature, where the active, and, as far as we are concerned, hidden powers, strive after and attain to a definite and settled form, from the crystallization of stones, to the conception and animation of animal bodies. This is life, or the motion of life in Space. It also exists in Time, where the motion itself constitutes life, from the beating of the heart to the periodical revolution of the planets in Space. Here and there an inner power expresses itself externally, and becomes visible, whether this be when in the act of perfecting itself, or when recognisable as an already perfected product seemingly in a state of constant quiescence.

Motion in Space is visible and exists for the eye; that in Time, on the contrary, is audible; and wherever life is present in Time it is perceived, as far as may devolve upon the sense, by the ear. Thus something dwelling within makes itself known in the Visible and Audible, and for the reason that that which becomes manifest is not the body itself, but the active forces within it, and an invisibility which we term Spirit, this manifestation is Spiritual. This spirituality operates through form, inasmuch as it fills Space, and also through tones, inasmuch as it renders possible a contemplation of Time. This latter constitutes the tone life of Nature, which, although perhaps not always perceptible to the human ear, is still a revelation of the inner spiritual existence, which pervades everything and is itself the Spirit of Nature.

§ II.

THIS is the spiritual principle of all life, inasmuch as it is given to every single creature in unchangeable mutual relationship with every other; and because it suffers and imparts influences, it is termed Sensibility, whether it be the pure sensibility of plants and animals, or that associated with reflection in mankind. The life which obtains in the creations of Nature, is, therefore, always full of sensibility; Death alone is without it.

Through this we have gained a closer view of the matter, for it follows from that which has already been said, that in living Nature generally—wherever life is present—an inner power arising from Sensibility becomes manifest. Although we cannot precisely define, or even comprehend the peculiar spiritual existence of each and every form of Nature, still it is everywhere present where life appears, and produces motion, or is implanted within it, and it expresses itself in sound and tone. The great Whole and all its parts sound in the same—without being perceptible to our limited senses—everywhere and for ever where life stands out through sensibility, and thus an inner spiritual condition becomes manifest through motion in Time. If a living creature, moved by others, and influencing them in return, attains to the expression of inner conditions, it also becomes perceptible in Tones.

§ III.

It will perhaps be remarked that the erroneousness of the above statement is quite obvious, seeing that Tones are nothing else than Motion in Space, either direct or resulting from air-waves produced by oscillating bodies, these merely being conditions of Space. And true it is that air in vibration constitutes the medium through which the Time-life of Nature is made perceptible to us, and that it exists in space; still, that which an inner life makes known to us, in these conditions of space, by means of the senses, is, as far as the sense of hearing is concerned, only temporal, and we regard as the spirit of the same not the moving air, not the corporeal air-waves, but through them the progressive motion in Time. Even the existence of such vibrations has been recognised by the eye only, and the science of Physics teaches us that the individual impressions only become perceptible by their frequent repetition.

If therefore the physical analysis of tone refers it to the vibrations of elastic bodies and of the air, so, from a metaphysical point of view, to tone is given an inner life, in which the accumulative corporeal tones are incorporeal, and effect more than the mere excitation of the nerves. Even, may we say that the life of sounds and tones tears itself from the body and becomes the purest of phenomena. From the point of view from which we now regard the matter, only the purely audible, which is temporal, is taken into consideration. The wind murmurs, the wheels of a coach rattle, a pistol-shot resounds simply as a concussion of the air; for not every sound is to us the expression of an independent life, although it must be confessed that a free Spirit, elevated above the human sphere, may regard as being animated, and as taking part in the universal harmony, an infinite number of Nature's phenomena, which we are accustomed to regard simply as mechanical productions, and are unable to refer to spiritual animation. When we speak of the tones and music of Nature, we understand thereby a direct or indirect manifestation arising from self-energy.

§ IV.

HAVING seen that in tones and their motion an inner life expresses itself, and constitutes the tone life of Nature, we are next led to inquire more closely into the character of Tone and Rhythm, having already anticipated, by hinting that tone is not regarded by us simply in the light of an External. It being foreign to the subject in hand, the reader must seek elsewhere for an explanation, in accordance with physical laws, of the nature of the disturbed air and its motion; here only the result of such investigation will be made use of, in order to show how the Temporal element of life melts into the Spacial, and the Spacial into the Temporal, and that they both obey similar laws; how the motion of the air becomes the expression of the moved Soul, and again operates upon the nerves, in order to be recognised in its similar and continuous motion. Sounds and tones are, to us, not merely arbitrarily selected signs, but the direct expression of inner life, and are products of Nature bound by a law of inner necessity. We must not overlook the fact that the nature of music may be regarded from two different points of view, either as *produced*, or originating within us, or as *received* and reaching us through the sense of hearing. In the one case the effect of music has to be taken into consideration, in the other the cause and origin of the same. In both respects the Visible forms an antithesis. Light illumines the world and discloses to us all visible existence, so that being enticed by objects, we draw nearer to them and comprehend them. Tone, on the contrary, brings the world to us, and causes it to penetrate within us, and to continue to live there. Both, by a power of comprehension, are perceived and appreciated, although language has but one word to express the two relations, describing as *contemplation*, the comprehension of both Spacial and Temporal forms.

From what has already been said it appears that that which we perceive in tones does not wholly depend upon corporeal contact, nor is the ear the ultimate resort. An inner susceptibility of spirit constitutes the perception, and a spirituality constitutes that which is perceived. And thus we have to consider a temporal existence, in which the change—the variation in rising and falling—proceeds from an inner principle, and strives to attain to the unity of ideal contemplation.

§ V.

OF TONE.

THOSE things which, from the observations of mankind, it was found necessary, at an early date, to distinguish one from another, language has fixed by a varied nomenclature; but ordinary usage by failing to observe the precise properties of words, and by confounding them, has placed considerable difficulty in the way of a clear comprehension. Therefore, in order to enable us the more readily to explain the various phenomena of the province of tones, and also to avoid misunderstandings, we must proceed to define certain related ideas.

Definite and indefinite sounds* are in a general way the effects perceived by the ear, and we thus describe that which, by the motion of air-waves, affects more or less powerfully the nerves of the body, and more particularly those of the ear. We thus speak of a

---

* In order to maintain the necessary distinctions, it was considered advisable to translate certain words which occur in this and the following sections thus:
        Laut—definite sound.
        Schall—indefinite sound.
        Klang—musical sound.
The English language contains no equivalents.

dull sound, of a piercing or clear sound. Whether the vibrations are regular or irregular does not here come under consideration, nor does the great variety of sounds, arising from the differences of composition in the bodies which produce them, affect this general idea. To distinguish between definite and indefinite sounds by reasoning that the former are assigned to an organic voice, does not affect the main issue, nor does it find confirmation in an universal usage.

Sound, when considered with reference to the vibrating body and its more or less regular vibrations, is called musical, and we rightly say a string sounds musically, and regard a pure or impure musical sound as a sound whose vibrations are, or are not, ordered by rule. A tone is necessarily a musical sound, but not every musical sound is a tone. When indefinite and definite sounds are heard, but, by reason of their uncertainty and irregularity, cannot be comprehended, but appear confused and unclear, we call the effect noise, just as noisy music may be spoken of as incomprehensible. This effect when greatly enhanced becomes clamour and uproar.

Tone is a musical sound by self-energy, and with certain relations. Thus definite and musical sounds may become tones if, being produced by self-energy, they enter into certain relations one with another; and even a single definite sound becomes a tone if we imagine it in relation to others, and to all tones, for instance, as being high or low, or as distinguishable by name.

Herein lies the essential character of tone, and not in the simultaneously sounding harmonics, as Rameau, and others before Chladni, took for granted; this admixture, on the contrary, robs the tone of its higher determinate character. Of these distinctions, the usage of ordinary life takes no account, and thus people speak of the good tone of an instrument, of a chord composed of three musical sounds (Dreiklang), and so forth, but thereby the matter is but little prejudiced. In scientific language, however, we must demand greater precision.

§ VI.

DEFINITE and musical sounds result from the vibrations of elastic bodies, or elastic masses; these vibrations being conveyed to the ear by the air and air-waves. In a space devoid of air no sound can be heard or produced. Upon the variety of the spacial properties of bodies depend the peculiarities of their vibrations, and consequently of their sounds; this is taught by that branch of natural science termed Acoustics, whose province it is to explain the laws by which vibrations are produced and made known to the ear; whereby a relation between the vibrations and this perceptive organ becomes apparent. But an inner quality is ever prominent, which forms itself to an external phenomenon in Time,—as it were tearing itself free from the corporeal. Then every vibrating body exhibits its own peculiar power of producing musical sound, inasmuch as a particular elasticity gives rise to a particular modification of the vibrations, just as, on the other hand, the comprehension of a certain motion is possible to the ear, or, by reason of imperfect formation, is denied to that organ. If then the whole of Nature exists in motion, and in vibrations which are sometimes perceptible, and sometimes incomprehensible to the human ear, we must acknowledge the existence of an universal tone-life in the great Whole and all its parts, and also, that every thing that lives has its own sound and its own voice. To a higher Spirit, which may be able to perceive more than man, the whole world must sound; and thus Pythagoras could speak of the music of the spheres, and Jean Paul, the poet, could hearken to the enchanting sounds of the blossoming trees, and the melody of the opening buds. Only in lifeless Nature does silence prevail, and the rest of Death knows no sound. In the sounds of Nature many different properties may be distinguished, in the illustration of which we may make use of analogies from the perceptions of the other senses, and speak of a clear, dull, thick, thin musical sound. But this we need not here take further into consideration; rather must we employ ourselves in elucidating what it is that converts musical sound into a tone. If we prosecute our inquiries with regard to the creation of tone, three points for consideration will arise.

§ VII.

(1.) A MUSICAL sound, which always constitutes a manifestation of inner properties, is either excited from without, or proceeds immediately from an inner spontaneity; although in life the boundary which divides the two is not clearly defined, and therefore a precise distinction is impossible. In the above distinction we recognise the first important token according to which we described Tone as a musical sound resulting from Spontaneity. This we fix by means of language. We obtain from a string a musical sound, but the human voice gives tone, and so does an instrument voluntarily excited by us. Mankind fashions the musical sounds of the twitched string or the blown flute into a succession of tones, and expresses his feelings therein; then from the instrument human tones are heard, a human voice; on the other hand, the gusts of air midst the strings of an Æolian harp produce now musical sounds, now an analogy to melody.

(2.) All sound belongs to time, and whatever of a spacial nature may cleave to it is not comprehended by the sense to which sound is given, but is gained by reflection, or by comparative observations of different kinds, and by combinations with that which is really perceptible to the sense of hearing. The ringing bell, the vibrating string, set in motion by the hand of man, are consequently not recognisable in their sounds as visibilities. Only the Temporal falls within the sphere of the Audible, and Chladni's sound figures represent nothing more than the moving segments of the sheet of glass between the nodes of rest. If a certain fixed relation of time is associated with the rhythm, and a regularity appears, then the sound becomes tone. Every tone depends, as phenomenon of life in Time, upon the fixed relations of a regular rhythm, and the laws of rhythm are, as later investigations have shown, identical with those of tone formation. Here we shall in nowise be embarrassed by the question whether the rhythmical is not also observable in Space, seeing that the flight of a bird, the motion of a galloping horse, have been termed rhythmical. The eye sees nothing more than spacial relations, and whatever of a temporal character is attached to, or blended with them, is merely the result of reflection. If in the gallop of a horse, or in a dance, rhythm shall be perceptible, then the sounding beat of the pulse, or the sound of the footstep must be added, or if this term shall also hold good for spacial motion we must accept a double meaning of the word. The vibrating string is in itself no tone, nor does it give tone until it audibly vibrates in a certain time, and the vibrations similarly succeed one another, when, in short, the objective precision is maintained in the subjective comprehension.

Though the power or weakness of a tone may be dependent upon the greater or less degree of the elasticity of the body, and its vibrations, and though a bell standing with its mouth upon the ground may sound as little as lead, yet this will not define the tone as such, for here we have nothing to do with spacial relations, and do not seek for the tone *in something*, but, rather, regard it as a manifestation independent of the corporeal. In such a case the body which is moved or vibrates comes no longer under consideration, but only the life which moves within it, which becomes a temporal phenomenon. This phenomenon is so independent in character that we do not inquire after the body which is visible to the eye, but believe in an existence which is not merely confined to space.

(3.) Sound is perceptible as a Difference and thus becomes Tone. As light in its indifferent condition is not recognisable as such to the eye, but becomes colour, and thus must enter into a Difference, and an Antithesis, so is it with Sound, which as Indifference is not recognisable as Tone. We perceive and comprehend a tone when the relations of acuteness and depth, of strength and weakness are added. Even a single tone maintains this difference, both with regard to a second tone, and to the tones which sound with it (overtones), the existence of which has long been acknowledged in the case of strings and is undeniable as regards wind instruments. In the music of mankind the different tones combine again in unity and form harmony. Height and depth, strength and weakness, constitute the third important point for consideration, which in so far coincides with the second, that the rhythmical laws are at the same time the laws for the various vibrations in a certain time. We call a tone high when the vibrations or air-motions are many and follow one another rapidly, and low when they succeed each other but slowly. The character is modified by the length of the body, and in such a manner that the acuteness of tone is in inverse ratio to the vibrating body, as the long and short strings of the pianoforte show. Two strings of equal substance vibrate and sound differently when their lengths are different. But the tension and thickness must also be taken into consideration, for a tightly strained and thin body vibrates quicker and sounds more acute; also by the strength of a body a greater rigidity and thereby more rapid vibrations can be produced; thus, for instance, a thin and not too stiff oboe reed gives the lower tones more readily than does a thick one.

A tone is called strong or weak when, through the various degrees of elasticity, a greater or less extent of vibration is induced, whereby it appears that an increase and decrease of motion in a certain ratio, is observable in the successive air-waves, to which we have an analogy in the case of colour; we therefore call it colour of tone.

The Difference, however, in which a tone appears must be definable and susceptible of an unity. Even in the case of musical sounds we distinguish purity as the unity of similar vibrations, for the reverse of this is noise.

§ VIII.

ON these particulars depends tone, which we regard as the spontaneous manifestation of an inner life, in rhythmical relations, and in difference to a diversity. It would not suffice were one to limit the nature of tone to the regularity of vibration, for by this alone a spiritual life could never become manifest. On the other hand, it may be well to offer a word of warning against attributing to the nature of tone that which the human mind develops from it by reflection, and then discovers in music; an error through which some have been led to regard the phenomenon of tone in such an abstract light, that not only all connection with the corporeal basis of sounding objects is disregarded, but it is made a purely ideal phenomenon, and is volatilized. We must not lose sight of the real foundation, however strongly we may attach ourselves to a spiritual importance. Before we turn to regard the boundary line which separates that which is human in the world of tones, we must more closely define the nature of rhythm and the ratio of differences in tones.

§ IX.

RHYTHM.

BUT few words have, by their improper use, led to so many misconstructions as has the word Rhythm, which, derived from a foreign language, should have enjoyed the positive application of a technical term. It will therefore be necessary to explain the various uses of the word. But we must observe beforehand that rhythm is not peculiar to human art, but belongs to the whole tone world, and that it is observable in the simplest phenomena of Nature, before all art, in which it becomes Beautiful rhythm.

Numerous have been the later attempts to explain in a definition the nature of rhythm, and it appears that almost every one has been successful in grasping the truth from his own point of view, without having secured for himself the right of rejecting the opinions of others. It was readily agreed that rhythm falls to time and its accomplishment, for by the generally accepted signification of the word, we understand the accented division and continuance of time by something perceptible, as illustrated, for example, by the sound of footsteps or the tick of a pendulum. A proportional recurrence of the sound causes the progressive time to become perceptible ; and if this term has been applied to spacial motion it has always been so in an improper sense. The province becomes narrower when we speak of musical rhythm and distinguish it from the metrical, however similar the laws of both may be. The former belongs to sounding nature and art, the latter to the human art of language. Both are based upon similar principles, for that which forms the metrical rhythm constitutes merely the musical element of language.

If we regard together the most important signs by which rhythm, in the strict sense of the word, becomes distinguishable to us, it will appear, as it always has appeared, that rhythm converts to an unity the combined sums of certain and various divisions of time, whereby it must be taken for granted that the time is filled and not empty, for void time cannot be perceived. Whatsoever appears in time must present itself under the form of divisions of time, and only in its divisions is time intuitively comprehended. Different parts, whether they are such by length or shortness, or by strength or weakness, form in rhythm a whole, as does proportion in space, wherefore the typical term time-figure, borrowed from spacial contemplation, may not be unsuited to its expression. That which it is here necessary to comprehend may be thus illustrated for clearer contemplation.

The roar of a waterfall and the Æolian harp, have for us little or no rhythm,—although it cannot be denied to either—but soar above the province of human comprehension, not carrying sufficient decision within them. Still variety is requisite. A single musical sound offers no rhythm; to develop this at least a pause must occur between the sound and its repetition. Two tones form a rhythm within the narrowest bounds; several sounds a complete rhythm. But even multifariousness is not sufficient. Perfectly equal divisions of time in continued succession, as produced by the blows of a hammer, or the swings of a pendulum, evince observance of law, and if it be found convenient to regard these equal motions, by reason of their separate parts, as rhythmic, and thus, for instance, to speak of the rhythm of a pendulum, then, at least, the coercion must be recognised ; on the removal of which at the entry, or rather at the return, of a diversity of rhythm, this latter attains to perfect validity. This rigid observance of rule is only observable in life that is not free, or in an imposed necessity, such as is nowhere found in Nature, or at least only in cases where the mechanical predominates. We must not, therefore, assume, as is too frequently done, that diversity develops itself from similarity, for it is a primitive condition. Nevertheless we may speak of a primitive agitation which is so constituted that, the divisions of time being equal, the one makes itself intensively prominent and the other recedes. If diversity be wanting in this coerced equal division of time, it is intensively gained by the heightened power, that is by accent, or whatever we may choose to term the differences of enhanced or greater power, expressed by musicians as strong and weak divisions of time, or Thesis and Antithesis, and by writers on metric as Arsis and Thesis.

The questions which now arise are : What may the principle of this arrangement of the various divisions of time effect in rhythm ? How does this variety become an important requisite of rhythm ? How can we explain the origination of a Thesis after, or out of an Arsis, and the combination of the two ? These discussions have been so disunited and so directly opposed to one another by scientific enquirers, who, as already stated, were for the most part agreed upon that which has hitherto occupied our attention, that this province may well be likened to a battle-field. However, more misunderstandings than errors have obtained on these subjects, or, at all events, the latter have resulted from the former. Almost all have, to a considerable extent, grasped the truth, and each individual has busied himself in denying it to others. Mutual respect and assistance would have brought the goal nearer than has a polemic which has often disregarded the right.

The first scientific foundation was laid by Hermann, who pointed out the principles of rhythm in a reciprocal operation, or rather in the relation of cause and effect. This was misunderstood and misinterpreted, for some denied the reciprocal operation because the divisions of time do not operate from both sides positively and negatively upon one another, a simple causal relation alone being in force; others pointed out the perfect accordance of cause and effect, as though an equality of the time-divisions could be demanded, which would entirely destroy the character of rhythm. Truly the idea of cause and effect appears too universal, and the expression *reciprocal operation* errs against the usage of language by which it applies only to a simultaneous presence: but even Apel himself, after a not exactly thorough refutation, was forced to recognise a causal relation. This learned man attempted a more precise explanation and laid down the proposition—Rhythm is the sensuous contemplation of the unity of a succession of moments of evolution; but thereby advanced, in the main, nothing more than did Hermann's Causality, although the indications may be of a more general character, for in Evolution, and in the Generation and Generator alluded to we perceive nothing further than a cause arising from an effect. Where the process allows us to recognise a progression into some state or condition, the mind naturally conceives a relation of cause and effect.

Through Apel a substantial indication, not thoroughly grasped by himself, was obtained of an existence appearing in temporal form. But the problems—to what extent the diversity in the coerced divisions of time, which by no means first makes its appearance in association with Beauty, may become an essential of rhythm; and how, in the constant progressive development, an increase and diminution of power is possible:—remained unsolved. At a more recent date errors again arose from a belief that rhythm, in its primitive condition, contained the Beautiful, disregardful of the fact that not every rhythm is beautiful, nor wholly a matter of art. All were content to see in this beauty nothing further than variety and its unity, through which alone, however, it cannot be produced. A solution of the problem was arrived at by deliberating as to what is afforded by a beautiful rhythm, which is doubtless a freedom from monotony and flatness, but as to how such variety exists, and is attained to, whether arbitrarily, or by rule, they did not trouble themselves. That which at a recent period was advanced by Hoffmann (Science of Metrik, Leipzig, 1835) as a fresh foundation, did little more than give other names in place of those which had been hitherto adopted. According to his theory, rhythm, which in its very nature is beautiful, consists in the alternation, in accordance with the law of exertion and recovery, of consecutive divisions of time, in which a strong and a weak exertion may be distinguished. All this Fries (" Philosoph. Æsthetics; or, Practical Philosophy," part ii. p. 236) had already taught, and if only by indications, still much more thoroughly. From the afore-mentioned theory we do not learn what occurs if, after an exertion, recovery does not immediately follow, but instead of it a further or enhanced exertion, neither are we told what it is that forms and arranges the various longs and shorts, nor what the prime reason for it all may be. Truly, the latter is pointed out in the necessity for antithesis which appears throughout Nature, but hereby we gain nothing more than an empty formula of the most recent school of philosophy.

§ X.

WE have already seen that in tones an inner motion of life expresses itself, through that which has motion in Time. Time takes up the tone as a Continuum, and this would constitute an ever-sounding Continuum, if an inner life did not assert itself, and if the form of the tone-motion were not also the form of the inner life motion. The inner life, however, consists, inasmuch as one effort determines the other, in the reciprocal operation of active forces, and, indeed, not altogether in manifold agitation, but in the alternate play of excitement and calm, which latter, however, by no means constitutes absolute rest. Expression and image of this inner life are the tones which become audible, which rhythmically unite and arrange themselves, inasmuch as they fill time in perceptible alternation, just as the inner life, as a Temporality, exists in rhythmical relations. The prime free reason for the rhythmical motion of tone is consequently contained in the inner life; from it the excitement proceeds; it determines the commencement, the change, and the expiration of the motion. The form of the phenomenon and of the manifestation is throughout of a temporal nature, and is a combination in which the subsequent is always dependent upon the antecedent, the present determined by the past. At the same time, however, both an alternation of activity and varying degrees of power are requisite, for if the former be wanting, a monotonous rest results, which may be compared with death, and progression is only possible by renewed excitement. An equal motion, like that of a pendulum, allows, as already observed, only a coerced life to be supposed, and is therefore only to be observed in the mechanical; it offers regularity, but no rhythm. When therefore some assumed, in respect of this, a Causality,

OF THE MUSIC OF NATURE IN GENERAL. 41

others considered the one effect to be produced by the other, it remained unexplained how this connection could arise from the effects themselves. That which here constitutes the operative, is the activity of the spiritual life which exists in collective Nature, as in mankind, the expression of which occurs in rhythm. In life, from strain and exertion proceed relaxation and rest, and the second result of activity cannot be greater than the first. That Causality which obtains in our own inner life is also observable in tones, and is the modifying principle.

§ XI.

THE simplest excitement of living motion consists, by equality of time divisions, in an intensive concentration of power, whereby one part is made prominent. This gives accented rhythm, in which the one equal part stands out through intensity of force, and the concentration repeats itself, thus: ╱ __ ╱ __ ╱ __ ╱ __ or ╱ __ __ ╱ __ __ ╱ __ __. But accent must not here be confounded with pitch of tone, but only the marked tone forming the boundary point of the time-figure must be understood. This concentration of power may appear in a double form, inasmuch as in the equality of parts, several, and in certain grades different, accents may exist and consequently a rhythm with various accents be produced ╱╱ ╱ __ or ╱╱ __ ╱ __ . This diversity becomes greater with the change of the duration of the time-divisions, or through the extensive relations of tones, which can give rise to a multitude of even and uneven divisions; thus, for instance, a long may be of equal value with two shorts, or with three or four shorts, and may be resolved into the same. The duration of these longs and shorts is not regulated by any law, and the sub-divisions may be carried to any extreme that their perception by the human ear admits of. That which extends beyond the natural capacity of that organ may well exist, but it is lost.

Although the understanding cannot find out and express the quantities, the feelings comprehend the unity of the rhythmical relation. Still for the human mind a limit is fixed, represented by the quadruple quantity, whether it be expressed musically by crotchets or semiquavers. Even that which exists immediately beyond this quantity in the number five, although still comprehensible to the feelings, is not pleasing, and it is difficult to obtain, by the accentuation of the first division, a balance between one and five, or to realize the unity of five divisions. A septuple arrangement is still more objectionable to the feelings, and rhythms of 11, 13 and 17 divisions are quite disagreeable and useless. Therefore Leibnitz was justified in asserting that the human ear can only count up to five. The relations 1-2 and 1-3 are the most natural and most usual.

It does not appear necessary to enumerate the

various forms of the association of longs and shorts, for even though the combination should evince a greater or less degree of freedom, still the characteristics of rhythm remain in each case the same. Let it, however, be remarked, how vain was the contention between writers on metric and musicians when the latter bitterly complained that the former, starting from the assertion that a long is equal to two shorts, confined themselves to the long (—) and short (⏑) and did not point out in the newly-invented notation a difference of various shorts : ♩ . ♩ ♪♪ ♪ or ♩ . ♪ ♫ ♪. for example. The relative proportions of length do not induce an alteration of form as far as metrists are concerned, and as rhythm (metric) associated with language only presents itself in art productions, it must be admitted that a proportion of 1-3 is therein only permissible conditionally and in transition. Recently metrists have conceded a duple rhythm, with which musicians may rest content, and recognise with the ancient rhythmists the existence of an irrational long, which does not quite contain two divisions, and admits that a long syllable may be lengthened by a half, thus :—
— ⏑ ⏑ ⏑ which is equivalent to ♩ . ♪♪♩ When however, they are disinclined to regard with musicians the triole ♪♪♪ as equivalent to ♩., the justification exists in language which is confined to the simpler and more easily comprehended relations.

§ XII.

IF a rhythm contain a Whole, this, although divided into moments of time, has an end, but no break. But during the undisturbed progress of time, a break may occur in the tones which fill it, and thus a moment void of tone may occur. Through this, however, the rhythmical relation is not disturbed, inasmuch as the time unfilled by tone is also included in the time series. This is the pause which at certain points prevents the filling of time, but does not destroy the rhythm. The duration of the pause may be equal to that of a long or a short, and it obtains to rhythmical importance through the rhythm, which is in the main apparent, and in which it takes part. It has been asserted that within a rhythmical succession a pause cannot occur, but only between two rhythms, which unite to form a single series; yet within the series, there is an interval which falls to the recovery succeeding the exertion, and which, although void of tone, s still of importance, and does not occasion a break. What are so-called staccato, or briefly sustained notes ♪ ⌐ ♪ ⌐ ♪ ⌐ but a rhythm with pauses interspersed? Such do not destroy rhythm.

§ XIII.

No one has ever doubted that rhythm belongs to Time, and consequently to Tone-life; it has, however, often been questioned whether tones and music occur absolutely under the form of rhythm. Gottfried Weber has declared rhythm to be a not wholly indispensable property of music, giving an illustration of music without rhythm. This assertion, however, arises from a misunderstanding, by which rhythm is mistaken for musical time, or the strictly preserved norm of equal rhythm, and when Weber quotes, as an illustration, and compares with recitative, the ordinary choral song of the community, in which the longer or shorter duration of tone does not strictly conform to musical time, but is, so to say, arbitrary, it is evident to us that only time is absent, and not rhythm. Of musical time we shall have occasion to speak elsewhere. It is evident that a sound, in itself, is wanting in rhythm, but when it participates in certain relations it becomes tone, and when combined with others in a series, exhibits rhythmical form, and thus wherever tones exist in combination, the law of rhythm obtains.

§ XIV.

THE RELATION OF TONES IN ACUTENESS AND GRAVITY.

BETWEEN tones, by reason of the various degrees of rapidity of the vibrations, a difference arises, which is termed Interval. The length of the vibrating body, its substance and tension, determine the number of air-waves which, striking upon the organs of hearing, constitute acute or grave tone. How it is brought about that the sounding body vibrates, and that the air-waves act upon the organs, and excite the sensations, is for that part of Physics termed Acoustics to determine and explain. If the vibrations follow one another at equal intervals, then, instead of mere sound, a tone is produced which has a certain pitch. In a certain sense the deeper tone, resulting from slower motion, can be regarded as the compact unity of the diverging higher tones, so that we may say, these proceed from the deeper fundamental tone. But, on the other hand, the more acute tone is equal to the graver, for the reason that by increased motion, it gains in number what it loses in fulness. Thus the octave is equal to the prime, and yet different from it.

The compass within which tone exists, must be regarded as of infinite extension; even within the limits of the human comprehension it is still very large, extending, according to Wollaston, over ten octaves. The 32 feet C of the organ, which vibrates 32 times in a second, and the C which vibrates 16,384 times in the same length of time, may be regarded as the extremes; but Weber has shown that air-waves of all kinds produce sound, when not less than 15 and not more than 30,000 vibrations reach the ear in a second. The proportions of the successive tones recur again in an enhanced state, but still the same, in the octave, so that within an octave we can comprise all intervals. But as acuteness and gravity are only relative ideas, and the difference of tones is infinite and scarcely definable, so it occurs that from a desire for a fixed starting point, we proceed to judge all tones in accordance with the organisation of the human ear, and to arrange their relations. It is not for us to discuss whether a differently constituted organisation, and another manner of comprehension, may not be able to appreciate other tone relations which with us have no value. We are not in a position to judge of the Nature beyond ourselves, otherwise than as it exists for mankind. Even where the Pleasing and the Beautiful are in question, we know that in the human province of tones, different periods and individuals are opposed to one another, and the relations which were recognised in ancient times, and in which the Asiatic and Northern races delighted, are perhaps useless to us, and displeasing to our ears. Man, as soon as he has attained to mental development, perceives and determines, in the relations which he is able to calculate by means of figures, a certain succession, such as is offered by the scale. This finds its application in Art. We shall return to it further on.

§ XV.

FROM what has hitherto been said, it will appear that everywhere, where tone becomes perceptible as the expression of an inner life, rhythm and the relation of acuteness and gravity forms the basis, and that therefore, these are present throughout sounding Nature, even when they cannot be estimated by the rules adopted in the music of mankind. In this form the Spiritual, which pervades the whole of the existence around us, is exhibited temporally, so that Nature, in the broadest sense of the word, lives and appears in tones, and we may thus speak of the music of the world and of every single thing. But we may go still further in this investigation, and enquire—How is music made known in the circles of the living productions of Nature beyond the human sphere? What is the tone-life of Nature in contradistinction from human Art? Can we regard musical art as an imitation of Nature?

§ XVI.

THE MUSIC OF NATURE BEYOND THE HUMAN SPHERE.

IN regarding the vast range of the living productions of Nature, and enquiring in individual cases into the tone-producing faculty, and the capacity for music in the same, we must not fail to take every precaution against the possibility of error, for only too easily do we transfer human nature to other beings, and ascribe to Nature, from a poetical regard, as peculiarity and spontaniety, that which has a foundation only in our imagination; thus the poet hears songs in the murmur of the wind, and melody in the ripple of the brook. Even the assertion that the greater the power of a being to produce tone, the higher it stands in the scale of earth organisations, does not apply in general and in every case, for numerous well-founded experiences militate against it. This mystery of creation is concealed beneath a veil which we can raise only in certain places, and our glance never penetrates deeply enough into alien natures. Who would rank the docile and affectionate dog far below the not particularly intelligent nightingale? In general it will be found that the nature beyond mankind possesses only definite and indefinite sound, although its participation in the development of tones cannot be denied.

§ XVII.

THE world of the inorganic we do not call dead; it hides within the predominating mass of the body a slumbering life, and the forces which are able to create sounds and tones are not yet awakened; the tones themselves remain hidden in the immobile mass, to be awakened by a foreign impulse, when man makes it a means of his free purposes. The bodies of this sphere, which lack the power of producing notes spontaneously, are distinguishable one from another, by the greater or less degree in which they serve the purpose of producing human tones.

The noble metals distinguish themselves also in this respect, for they are better adapted to tone than are those which we regard as the inferior metals. In less dormant life the activity for tone production is enhanced. Truly, we are not in a position to comprehend by means of the organs of hearing the motion of the temporal plant life, which, without doubt, expresses itself in musical sounds, but we observe in the instruments derived from the vegetable kingdom, that the property which adapts them to the production of tone, is given to them in a higher degree of perfection than it is to those constructed of metal. This possibility of receiving spiritual animation points at least, to a kindred nature: still, to the, in itself, passive instrument we cannot ascribe anything further than the subordinate part above mentioned. If we pass upwards through the scale of living things, we find in the lower regions, at first, neither any apparent power of producing sounds which are perceptible to us, nor susceptibility to tones. The organs for both are wanting. Noises produced by outer portions of the body, as in the case of bees, crickets, and other insects, must not here be taken into consideration. Tone-life appears in the least degree of activity in fishes, amongst which a few species (Cottus cataphractus, Cobitis fossilis) produce sounds. Of animals of this low class authentic observations have been communicated which cause astonishment, for in the susceptibility for melody evinced by fishes and crabs, which followed a strain of music, a reproduction of that which was heard must be taken for granted. With the Amphibia, owing to the presence of the lungs, a development of voice and note commences, without, however, attaining to musical importance, for however various in this respect the individual species of animals may appear —and a number of the class Mammalia occupy a low position—others by a participation in music that becomes audible to them, distinguish themselves in a remarkable manner, as was observed in the well-known concert for two elephants at Paris (vide *Musikalische Zeitung*, 1799, No. 19)—still it is generally recognised, that, in the voice of the bird, which amongst animals alone sings, we first meet with that which may be regarded as music. Here again a poetical conception, not seldom causes persons to ascribe to Nature that which is quite foreign to it, and, for instance, to hear in the notes of the quail the words Lobe Gott, (syllabically rendered in English " Praise the Lord ") and in the trill of the lark a hymn in celebration of spring, and otherwise to interpret symbolically the sounds of Nature. It is not everything in this sphere, which, possessing a voice, can produce music. Where the power of self-energy does not make itself known, nor that which is inward and spiritual express itself, tones are but the result of external circumstances, or of a corporeal, but not free activity. Just as the flute clock, by means of a mechanism which in itself is dead, performs even works of art, the action which mechanically repeats them being but the product of human ingenuity, so the song of birds lacks the expression of a free inner life, for they sing mostly at a time when they are influenced by sexual instinct. We can, therefore, ascribe tones to them only as the product of a conditional spontaneity of low grade, in which perfect freedom is wanting, and consciousness, by choosing for its representation a fixed and distinguishable sign, does not operate decisively. Herein we may only recognise the product of instinct. But even when more closely regarded, these tones are, from a musical point of view, in many respects distinguishable from those of mankind. It is quite impossible to adapt them to our musical scale, and in vain do we attempt to express in notes, the song of birds, while all the laborious attempts from Athanasius Kirscher to the present time have led to no results. Although, in a certain sense, mathematically determinable proportions cannot be denied to it, still it oversteps the harmonic conditions which regulate human music, and which cannot be regarded as accidental. The variety and contrasts are great, inasmuch as from the fundamental tone much finer proportions are developed than our scale exhibits; they are, however, useless for the music of mankind, and cannot even be grasped with certainty by the human ear. What we perceive are but analogies.

The song of the bird is by no means deficient in rhythm, although it is not human or musical rhythm, but deviates from the laws which are valid with us, and oversteps our naturally arranged proportions. In particular the import of the pause is wanting, and although, for instance, the cuckoo may, in his song, repeat correctly the minor third, that person deceives himself, who with Busby (*History of Music*, part 1, p. 6) and others, maintains the existence therein of a precise accentuation, and strictly preserved pause. Also that, which in human music, produces as spiritual element the initial note (initial imperfect bar), must be looked for in vain, if we do not find in song, that is not human the application of the initial note,—for not every anticipatory note can be regarded in· this light. Blumenbach was therefore right when he said: "Birds do not sing, but merely whistle." It may be termed a species of music, but not human music. We cannot expect the latter where a perfect activity of the free spirit and of the feelings does not obtain. From the scream, as an expression of bodily suffering, to the song without words, the transition is not so easy as it appears; between them lies a power of spirit which must first be acquired, and which demands more than the mere play of physical powers. The experiences which have been adduced with reference to these matters lend no small interest to the confirmation, although, perhaps, they are not sufficiently explicit to lead to any decided results.

The song of the thrush consists of five or six parts, and the last note of each part is a sort of after-note (nachschlag) without harmonic close, such as cannot be made use of in music. The blackbird has a decided rhythm, which may be variously regarded, but it cannot, without alteration, be adapted to our metrical system. However admired the song of the nightingale may be, and however delightful its lively play of tones, still it moves in no musical rhythm, and after long sustained notes, not seldom a number of short notes follow, or an irregular shake, which is apt to degenerate into a scream.

The mocking-bird (Turtus polyglottus), native in America, is regarded by naturalists as the most excellent of all singing birds, as master of his art. According to J. Renunie (*Magazine of Natural History*, No. 5, 1829, compare Frioreps' *Notizen*, 1829, No. 519), and Audubon (*Ornithology of America*, compare *Morgenblatt*, 1832, No. 84), it possesses on the one hand, a large compass, and much variety in a full voice that modulates with remarkable ease, resembling the song of the nightingale, but without the long sustained tones, and on the other hand, a power, developed to an extraordinary degree of facility, of imitating the sounds of Nature, such as, for instance, the murmur of the leaves, and of the brook, and the songs of other birds, blending them with its own, so that one imagines to hear, first a linnet, then a partridge, then an owl, a duck, or a hen; but all this does not constitute musical discernment, and the mocking-bird may be likened to a man who has the gift of imitating the sounds produced by all kinds of animals.

§ XVIII.

THE tones of beings other than man are, therefore, not musical. This is confirmed by all observations adduced by naturalists, according to which certain rhythmical musical relations are recognisable, but are in nowise fit to be classed among the fundamental forms developed by the human mind. If we cannot, strictly speaking, call this music, neither can we speak of the music of Nature. Nevertheless, that which moves in such irregular intervals and which cannot be referred to the strict rules of musical time and harmony, is a song, and does not displease us; on the contrary it is charming and interesting. We can only form a judgment on this point, when we remember when and under what circumstances music appears. This only happens when spiritual freedom is spontaneously exhibited, and governs the expression of an intellectual life. Freedom carries with it its own laws, with which it dominates, freely creative, over the Necessitated and the Restrained; therein a spiritual life manifests itself, which stands forth from within as a free nature, and makes known the self-efficient comprehension and clear consciousness of an independent existence. The tones of Nature are, therefore, not music in the sense accepted by mankind, for freedom does not exist therein, and the kind of self-energy which is exhibited is invariably coerced. They are either created by an unconscious chance, and without spiritual activity, and combined without choice and arrangement, as in the case of the Æolean harp, concerning which one cannot say that the wind makes the music, or they express a sensuous perception of the instinct in which the necessity of Nature rules and compels. This perception Nature allows mostly to become audible in cry and shriek, for the reason that she is not master of it in consciousness. Then we perceive simply an analogy of feeling, such as is generally observable in the animal world. It is then physical impulse, sensuous desire arising from sexual instinct, that causes the bird to sing, not the expression of a purely spiritual condition, not of a conscious inner contemplation. When the lark mounts singing to the sky, and the finch and nightingale give note midst the foliage, is it not their delight and enjoyment of life that they make audible? Certainly it is the expression of a perception of life, but merely that of an ordinary life emotion bound by physical laws, the expression of corporeal enjoyment and of desire. In this respect the chirping sparrow, and the nightingale are alike; during the brooding season they are silent. Naturalness is evinced, but not intelligence. Luther judged quite correctly respecting the celebrated Josquin, in the following words: "His composition is right joyful, flows willingly, mildly, and charmingly, not forced and necessitated like the song of the finch, and, for all that, is quite according to rule."

§ XIX.

IF only that in which Spirit and Freedom prevail can give satisfaction to mankind, so we are informed as to what it is that in the tones of Nature pleases and satisfies us. We must, however, first separate that which is simply the result of imagination, as, for instance, the pleasure found in the shrill cries of a canary. As regards the rest, in which man finds himself referred to a more definite succession of tones and a more regular rhythm, it is the analogy to that which is free which delights, in the same way that the analogies of reason in animals of other sorts, obtain to human interest. Therefore either the purity of tone may delight, or the resentment of a free power to the restraint of Nature, or the resemblances which mix themselves therein without attaining to that which is human. We attribute to it also a spiritual animation, and confer upon the song of the nightingale the feeling of longing, or hear in the notes of the quail a religious utterance. In this symbolization, Nature, according to our ideas, serves us, but the image in alien Nature, which we grasp and draw nearer to us, is that of ourselves alone.

§ XX.

BUT here we stumble upon an assertion that is often repeated in the *History of Music*, and upon a law often adduced in Art-Philosophy, both of which seem quite antagonistic to that which has been stated above. History tells us that man doubtless received his first musical instruction from birds, and by imitation developed his song. Art-Philosophy proceeds from the fundamental law that man, as artist, is referred to Nature, and must imitate her in his works. That which man himself possessed there was no occasion for him to obtain by borrowing, and even if he did receive his tones from Nature, it was *his* nature, in the original possession of which, and in accordance with whose innate laws, he formed a representation for the expression of his inner life, so that the means which he grasped served him to exercise his intellectual faculties. Wherever in outer Nature he becomes aware of free motion, or even only of its resemblance, he sees in the same, living pictures, aye, copies for his representations. In that which is apparently unrestrained by law, or which deviates from rule, as, for example, the song of birds, he recognises a kind of free form, and can regard it as the expression of a freedom, which, however, he himself first attributes to it, although in itself it is but the product of an imposed necessity.

§ XXI.

MUSIC, if we do not yet subordinate the idea to that of Art, but merely avoid extending it indefinitely, is the property of man, and is of his creation. But

OF THE MUSIC OF NATURE IN GENERAL. 59

Nature has constituted him the creator. Music, therefore, no less than Poetry and Painting, is a product of the human mind, although it enjoyed an earlier existence, before reflection had created rules and theories to which art is subjected. The truth of these assertions is proved in a twofold manner. The so-called savage races, and even those which are simply uncultivated, show us that music is first attained to with the fuller development of the intellectual faculties, and is not to be found where the preponderance of the physical, detracts from the activity of the mind. A second proof is offered in the effect of music upon beings not human, and upon the uneducated. Many animals cannot endure music, others hear it without pleasure. But those animals that are more nearly associated with mankind, although perhaps, of apparently inferior type, are enchained by music as by the magic of another world. Doubtless the experiments upon spiders (*Musikalische Zeitung*, 2nd year, p. 653), and other animals left much to be desired in the way of completion, and foundation, but still, even a collection of that which is scattered, naturally leads to more decided results.

Uncultivated nations are pleased partly by mere sound, and the sensations of life which induce them to cry out, even although the delight be derived only from the corporeal vibrations which the strongly moved air produces upon their bodies, and partly by rhythm alone, as is the case with the Scotch Highlanders, in whom the now roughly grating, now softly humming tone of the bagpipe, awakens encouragement or compassion simply by means of rhythm. But that cannot be termed music which merely sensuously arouses and affects us. Only in the efficiency of pure intellectual organization rests the possibility of perfect comprehension.

END OF CHAPTER THE FIRST.

CHAPTER II.

OF THE MUSIC OF MANKIND.

§ I.

THE contemplation of the nature of tones, and of the peculiarities of the tones of Nature, makes apparent to us a line of demarcation, by which, in the great Whole of the life which becomes audible, a certain sphere of humanity is separated from the rest. To this we are referred when we speak of music in the strict sense of the word, and subject it to æsthetical judgment. But before all the following questions must be answered:—In what does music, which we have termed a creation of mankind, consist? and what is purely human in the formation, order and combination of tones, such as are made use of by mankind in life and art? We will answer them by analysing the character of music and by pointing out the peculiarities of its separate features. The characteristic is threefold. We possess in music a product of free self-activity which was attained to by the progressive development of the reflecting intellect; we recognise in it the immediate representation of the activity of the feelings, and a Totality in which the activity of all powers of the soul combines for the representation of an *Art-Beautiful.*

§ II.

MUSIC THE PRODUCT OF FREE SELF-ACTIVITY OF THE MIND.

No blind instinct causes man to sing and to play music, as it is sung and played by him. In the period of development when he was merely given to natural pursuits, and had not attained to independent powers of mind, he possessed either no music at all, or an extremely poor music. It is reported of the Patagonians of South America, who are represented as being men of large stature, and great bodily strength, and adroit hunters, that they do not evince the slightest aptitude for music, and do not sing. Where culture has broken the fetters of a preponderating sensuousness, and the mind with spontaneous activity invents and arranges, there music steps in, and mankind with reason awakened, selects the sounds of Nature wherein to express the true likeness of his innermost life. Therefore our children sing, even in the cradle, better than grown-up savages and the uncultivated. When Guido d'Arezzo arrived in Bremen to instruct the people in church song, he wrote back to say that it was not in his power to advance music in the slightest degree, for the inhabitants sang like asses. The educational influence of society penetrates in an extraordinary degree. Isolated man possesses in his narrowed circumstances only sounds for his requirements, and the gratification of his longings; he is on the whole more dumb or less loud than are animals. Entered into the relations of sociability, where an intellectual existence in love, and mutual elevation to a world of ideas, is held out to him, he develops the life which is peculiar to him, and soon his inner nature in active spontaneity, seeks expression, and requires that another being equally animated shall comprehend it; is such a being not present, he enters into cross intercourse with himself and sings solely for the sake of singing and of being heard. In the paths of Nature he pursues intellectual purposes; the proffered means of expression and the expression itself are at the same time necessary and arbitrary. Here also reflection becomes the creator of that which is human. However, a methodical manner of thinking, and well ordered projects must not be taken for granted, for in life mankind reflects much, and for the most part undesignedly, and without becoming clearly conscious as to the purpose, and follows securely the promptings of his inner nature. Consequently mankind does not acquire music by the imitation of Nature, nor did the birds, as Ernst Wagner asserted, teach him to sing; nevertheless he tarries, while constructing and creating with his powers of mind, within the bounds and under the conditions of Nature, and receives from her hands the material for elaboration. Excited from without, mankind has in this respect also, developed the germ within him to a full and beautiful blossom, and has spontaneously created music—*his* music. This acquirement and the ability of production, occurs variously developed, according to the different grades of cultivation. Races, periods, and individuals, endowed with different talents, diverge from one another, differing in inclination, but always the same in one respect, namely, that an inner life with self-determination attains to expression, and a rule is laid down as a foundation.

§ III.

IF in music we regard more closely this self-energy of reflecting man, it first becomes apparent to us in the succession of tones. The formation and arrangement of tones, which we term tone-succession or tone-system, is determined by reflection,—is a product of the human mind. This becomes evident to us in two ways; firstly, because such an arrangement is not to be found in Nature, and secondly because we can trace its development in history. No other creatures of Nature have sung previous to mankind, nor do they sing after the manner of humanity, and the harmony of Nature is not the harmony of human art. However variously the organs are formed, still the relations of tones might be universally the same; but even among the nations of the earth, we find equal capacity and aptitude, but not equal development. Although men may imitate with considerable skill the songs of birds, still it never becomes human music; moreover, we are mostly deceived with regard to that which we imagine to be the same, for being accustomed to our own system of tones, we unknowingly transfer it to natural song. Similarly, the songs of savages are not adapted to our succession of tones, and freely developed races cannot make use of them external to the art work, and not even then should they in themselves not permit of it. Some nations have never succeeded in attaining to the fourth and sixth. The Scotch Highlanders, in common with the Indian and Chinese races, lack the fourth and seventh, and arrange their scale c d e g a c. If the musical scale existed in a fixed form in Nature, every one would be able to sing, and always in tune. The impure tone is also a perfect tone, but is an incongruity, and that which constitutes the relation of tones, one with another, is not taught by Nature, but is gained and adopted by reflection. The Swiss and Tyrolese possess in their song both the fourth and seventh, but when uneducated in our music seldom intone them purely, but sing the fourth too high and the seventh too low for our ears. When the difficulty of these intervals,—which every teacher of singing has opportunity of observing in the case of children—is accounted for by some (*vide* Seidel, in *Charinomos*, Part 2, p. 85,) in the supposition that they contain something not completely in accordance with Nature, an error obviously obtains. They are quite in accordance with Nature, but are the products of acute reflection, and are, consequently, only to be found where the finer development of the intellect, directed thereto, renders them possible. The fourth occupies a position on the confines of the tonal arrangements, and is drawn now to the higher, and now to the lower region, if sagacity does not remove this vacillation. Amiot, in speaking of the music of the Chinese, relates that European melodies sounded so disagreeable to them, that they held their hands to their ears. On the other hand, it is useless to attempt to represent in our notes, with strict accuracy, the melodies of the Chinese and of the Scotch Highlanders.

§ IV.

THE range of tones in Nature is of unbounded extent, and is composed of infinitely small parts,—a pliant material, but one which requires elaboration before it can be of use to mankind. In Nature, as the monochord shows, a number of proportions present themselves, with regard to which usefulness comes under consideration before all. To these proportions mankind lays down the bounds, according to the condition of his mind, which is also effective in fixing the audible, and arranges that of which he can make use; and thus the natural succession of tones becomes the musical, and although derived from Nature, is nowhere found in the same in its prepared and definite form. The right of man thus to regulate Nature requires no justification; it is primitive, and was conferred upon him with mind itself. On certain points no small difficulties stand in the way of the attainment of an unity, which is absolutely essential to the mind, and as, in this respect, a progressive development has become historical, that which is at present adopted, although owing its continued existence to general acceptation, must not be regarded as a perfect, and the only tone system. That which lies beyond the limits of the comprehensible (and the human ear cannot comprehend the proportions of all numbers) must remain for ever shut out. Yet how freely mankind chooses and regulates within this circumscribed province, the history of his development throughout the vastly productive existence of nations, teaches us. We find that at different periods, different systems of tones were developed according to the position taken up by the reflecting mind in the province of sensuous contemplation. By degrees the law of proportions obtained to decided power, until it became universally recognised; and if the historical records were not so faulty, it would be easier to point out the way in which the reflecting mind attained to the height from which music now asserts its laws. Before a theory was developed, the scale was constructed upon no firmer basis than a natural, more or less cultivated æsthetical judgment, the truth of which was afterwards confirmed by mathematical proof. We are accustomed to oppose our modern system of music to others, and more particularly to that of the ancient Greeks, and a modern writer (Kiesewetter, in his " History of the

Origin and Development of our existing Music,") has not only denied the historic probability that modern music had its origin in that of ancient Greece, or was formed after it, but has even gone so far as to declare the latter to be quite contrary to Nature, as Chladni had done before him. But ancient music was in no wise contrary to Nature, and could not be so, although it was less musical, just as the song of birds or the song of Nature must, as far as we are concerned, be regarded as unmusical in a greater degree, that is, insufficient for the representation of intellectual life. Although it must be admitted that modern music first began to prosper when it became separate from the Grecian system, still it remains undemonstrable that our system of music did not and could not grow out of that of the Greeks. Our insight into that which antiquity possessed and practised will always remain much obscured, still no one can boast of possessing historical information as to the beginnings of Christian music, and it is an undeniable fact that in the development of the great Whole of the matters of humanity, no leap has taken place, and in no case can we perceive a second commencement without a previous gradual development of the elements.

Only a reformation, improvement, or remodelling, distinguishes a new period from a more ancient. Who could entertain doubts as to the possibility of the further development of our modern music, or choose anew the paths for the period of commencement? Dreiberg alone could maintain (in his remarks upon the music of the Greeks, p. 15) that everything that does not coincide with the Grecian music is erroneous and objectionable. But even that which, in the music of the ancients, some are accustomed to regard as arbitrary, finds sufficient justification in the free development of the reflecting intellect, and an error observed at a later date cannot be denounced as a fault.

Historians, by carefully following the course of development, can point out the validity and even the necessity of the individual progressions, provided that they cautiously distinguish between the simple reflections of life, or matters of custom, and the doctrines of theorists which, in their subtlety, frequently find no application in life.

§ V.

THE Tetrachord which served the Greeks as a basis for their tone system, constitutes a natural foundation. No blind veneration for the Pythagorean quadruple quantity—however often the Pythagorean doctrine of numbers may have given rise in more recent times, and in the more detailed parts of the science of music, to objectionable definitions—was the cause of the invention of the Tetrachord, or as Chladni has it, of the confinement of music within unnatural limits. The Greeks by a mode of reflection which was, in itself, by no means incorrect, arrived at proportion through melodic, a method which experience confirms even at the present day. On this point the reader may compare Nägeli's system for the cultivation of singing.

In the Tetrachord rests the element of melody, which, however, cannot be regarded as sufficiently satisfactory when the harmonic attains to validity or predominates. In ancient times the fourth was termed συλλαβή because it contained the first combination of consonant tones (πρώτη σύλληψις φθόγγων συμφώνων) whereby we may observe in what a simple and natural way the investigation commenced. Further, no one can deny that the determination of the three genera, the diatonic, chromatic, and enharmonic, was correctly carried out as far as was possible, and to a conclusion—hereby, of course, we take not its exclusive usefulness into consideration. All must admit that the diatonic scale of the Greeks was laid down with perfect correctness, and has consequently always been retained; that within the compass of the fourth, four notes are included, which, seeing that the difference between the fourth and fifth is equivalent to $\frac{8}{9}$, or a pure second, comprise two tones and a half.

A foundation-stone for the erection was obtained by the determination of the octave 1 : 2. The whole was represented at first by seven tones in the Heptachord, and at a later date by the complete octave in the Octachord, in which the fourth was expressed by 3 : 4 and the fifth by 2 : 3. Inasmuch as the Greeks, in order to secure an absolute measurement of the tone, *i.e.* of the whole tone, chose $\frac{8}{9}$, which represents the difference between the fourth and the fifth, whereby the semitone amounted to 243 : 256, they obtained pure fourths and fifths such as we do not possess, but, on the other hand, their thirds were less pure; still, the major third of 64 : 81 although 80 : 81 higher than ours of 4 : 5, has not been rejected in our modern systems of temperament, as, for instance, in the case of Kirnberger and others. Therefore it must not, without consideration, be described as contrary to Nature, and improperly are the tones of trumpets and horns referred to, in proof thereof, as giving only pure thirds of 4 : 5, for it is well known that upon these instruments the sixth tone in the two-lined octave $\bar{\bar{a}}$, when compared with the interval we recognise, is too deep, while the tone $\bar{\bar{f}}$ is too high, in fact just as they occur in folks-song, for instance, in those of the Swabians. Nor can the acceptation of the whole tone 8 : 9 be regarded as contrary to Nature merely because there exists a smaller whole tone of 9 : 10. With thought, mankind sifts and arranges for his own purposes that which Nature proffers him. In the determination of the remaining genera, viz., the chromatic and enharharmonic, we may also recognise a free-minded combination, and the result of progressive reflection. The transformation of the one whole tone into a half tone so that $\frac{1}{2}$ 1 $1\frac{1}{2}$ succeed one another as the chromatic genus, and the splitting of the half tones into the quarter tones of the enharmonic genus, was not displeasing for the same reason that these intervals are now displeasing to us, nor, in so far, accidental and groundless that only the preservation of the Pythagorean quadruple quantity, in the idea not to tolerate more than four tones in the Tetrachord, had led to it. Here then was presented to the Greeks a fixed system in an usable condition, and in a then existing music far removed from all artificial theory, upon which—never having heard any antique music—we are not in a position to deliver a verdict of total rejection; while that which is erroneous, wherever it occurs, can only be ascribed to the imperfection or excessive subtlety of theoretical doctrines. Even the modern Greeks, at the present day, make use of nicer tone proportions than we are accustomed to perceive. Obviously it cannot be our intention to explain fully, or deliver judgment upon the old and new systems of the Greeks; our object was rather to show that the former had its foundation in Nature, that it constituted a fine combination of the reflection, and that regarded from the then existing point of view, it does not appear worthy of condemnation. These acknowledgements so often denied in one-sided arguments, could not be withheld in one of the latest attempts at a restoration. When Kretzschmer attempted—whether satisfactorily, or in detail worthy of approbation need not be taken into consideration—the development of tones by progressions of fourths, and the critics, with substantial reasons, defended the temperament of our music, they could not deny that this construction was based upon a fact of Nature, and carried out with sagacity.

§ VI

IF we follow the progress of development, it will appear that here also practice preceded theory, and did not accommodate itself to the demands of the same without mature consideration. To the strict canonicans, the harmonists opposed themselves, and moved for that which gives satisfaction to the ear. Both calculated, but the harmonists not without regard for the principle which governs the representation of human feeling. Amongst Grecian theorists Lasus is mentioned as having ascribed to tones a sort of temperament which he termed the breadth of the same, apparently in that sense, by which tone admits of an expansion according to the relations of the various keys. Didymus recognised the validity of the thirds of 4 : 5 and 5 : 6, and adopted for the small semi-tone the proportion 9 : 10, for the semi-tone 15 : 16 and 24 : 25. This fundamental improvement necessarily commenced as soon as the want of an adequate harmony was felt. Even the deviations of Ptolomeus, if we except a few errors, are not to be regarded as disfigurements, but as the preparation for a future reformation. The keys which had already been fixed, as various forms of the octave, were retained; for the scales of the Holy Ambrosius, differing in the situation of the semi-tone, are really only the ancient Greek scales; the first or Dorian mode (d e f g a b c d) contains the Phrygian, the second, Phrygian (e f g a b c d e) contains the Dorian, the third, Lydian, (f g a b c d e f) contains the Hypolydian, the fourth Mixolydian (g a b c d e f g) contains the Ionian arrangement of tones, although the sizes of the intervals were not quite equal. The province was extended towards the end of the sixth century, by Gregory the Great, who added to these four ecclesiastical modes, which were termed authentic, four others—the plagal modes—in the fourth below. For the choral of several parts which had become customary in the churches, the adopted keys were not sufficient as they were wanting in the subsemitonium, or the semitone below. History shows us for what a length of time the people hesitated between the adoption of a new system and the maintenance of the old, and inasmuch as freedom of thought could not be restrained by the rules adduced in theory, and as the productions of artists lay before them in esteemed and satisfactory examples, the theoretical rules were remodelled in accordance with the same. Harmony developed itself, and, with it, artistic invention, as the result of an investigation which attained to even greater perspicuity. In addition to the use of the octave, fifth, and fourth, that of the third and sixth—which if not wholly rejected by the ancients, were at all events disregarded by them—became, before all and with justice, perfectly valid; and thus a new system was attained to, which, if not laid down with strict mathematical accuracy, still, on the one hand, coincided with the use of the instruments which had been invented, and on the other adapted itself to the expression of that which was pleasing to the ear. A natural progress of development is also here apparent. Whether Guido d'Arezzo or a later theorist, perhaps one of Guido's pupils, constructed the Hexachord, or whether the doctrine was gradually developed under the co-operation of several, remains a question ; it is however undoubtedly a fact that a new grand epoch for music, and one of continuous development, commenced with the establishment of successions of chords, and the proper appreciation of thirds and sixths. Then the dissonances were added, and were used in transition, whence originated the more ancient kind of counterpoint (contrapunctus floridus). We must not overlook the fact that Guido greatly improved the method of notation, which in the 12th century first attained to the necessary decisiveness and facility of application, and thereby promoted, in no small degree, the study of music.

§ VII.

THE reflecting mind proceeded further. Until the 15th century music was confined to the octave, and knew no modulation into another mode, as the old melodies, " Herr Jesu Christ dich zu uns wend" by Huss (1400), " Nun ruhen alle Wälder" by Isaac of Prague (1480), remind us. Variety in melody and harmony was wanting. Centuries elapsed ere mankind allowed the structure of the collective tone system to rest upon the basis of the major and minor modes. The octave was divided into twelve degrees, so that there were twenty-four keys. But every tone could not be rendered perfectly pure, unless for every pure major and minor third, fourth, and fifth, a number of secondary strings were made use of, amongst which the quarter tones would also have found place. The tones presented by the monochord could not suffice for the requisition of such equal proportions, for even though it were tuned to the pure fundamental tone, the remaining tones did not produce amongst themselves pure proportions. Therefore, for the sake of simplicity, a temperament was chosen, and variations from purity of interval were allowed, that each of the twelve tones might be used as the fundamental tone of both major and minor, whereby, with purity of the remaining proportions, the minor third was represented by 27 : 32 instead of 5 : 6, and the fifth by 27 : 40 instead of 2 : 3, being consequently too small by 80 : 81 or the syntonic comma. Further, the major whole tone or major second appeared in a duple proportion of 8 : 9 and 9 : 10, a difference of a comma. Hence appeared the necessity for a compensating division,—for an equal temperament, in which the fifths were tempered the twelfth part of the comma lower, the fourths higher, and the purity of the thirds and sixths was affected to the extent of a third part of the comma (diesis), but in such a manner that, with the greatest possible exactitude in the distribution of the difference, the purity of the octave was preserved. In order to spare the simpler consonances, Kirnberger chose an equal temperament by which only the fifths d a, a e, and f♯ c♯ lose in purity. Others acted upon different principles, for instance, Keppler, Euler, and Stanhope. When therefore Chladni compares this temperament and the new tone-system with the ancient arrangement of tones, as that which is natural and secure, compared with that which is arbitrary and vacillating, he labours under a misconstruction, seeing that the elasticity of tone, and the pliancy of the sense of hearing which accepts an approximate resemblance to perfect purity, destroys mathematical proportion, while unity of opinion with regard to that which sounds well, cannot lay claim to universal validity. We can only admit that for instruments and for human voices cultivated in accordance with them, a canonic purity is not practicable, and that therefore temperament becomes necessary. For us the proportions represented by whole numbers, from 1 to 6, are consonant intervals, their proportions being readily comprehended, still they differ according to the degree of approximation (the fifth is more consonant than the third, the fourth inclines more towards dissonance); on the other hand, the variety is not quite reduced to an unity in the proportions which lie over 7 (minor seventh $\frac{7}{4}$ diminished fourth $\frac{7}{5}$); dissonant to us is the greater difference, in which unity is not clearly perceived, thus 9 and 15 (second $\frac{9}{8}$ and $\frac{10}{9}$ major seventh $\frac{15}{8}$). Accordingly the relations of 7 degenerate, and with regard to these intervals many doubts have arisen. Tartini, Euler, and Kirnberger argue for the usefulness of this proportion and call it i; Chladni, in the 35th part of *Cæcilia*, regards it as useless, because every tone would necessarily receive its i, and the pianoforte, the flute and other wind instruments, together with the notation, would require alteration,—reasons which are of no great weight, and which cannot even struggle against a "groundless speculation."

Fasch, on the contrary, in a Mottett allowed the chord, c, e, g, i to pass into that of g, d, g, h without displeasing, and violoncellists make use of the flageolet tone beyond g, which is perceptibly higher than a, and deeper than b flat. However much we may be inclined to recognise as sufficient that which we possess, to wonder at the peculiarly acute combination, and to reckon our arrangement of tones amongst the most successful results of human thought, yet the belief in the perfectibility of the tone system, has a foundation in the fact that it can but be regarded as a creation of the human mind, and that progressive sagacity will in the future still be able to evolve new ideas. In vain do acousticians struggle against the opinion that the scale which is valid with us, is the product of arbitrary selection, seeing that its basis is to be found in Nature rather; for upon this undeniable basis, reflection, without having previously perceived the foundation, raised a structure, the proportions of which could be afterwards pointed out. That, which in our tone system, has been arranged to the satisfaction of the ear, and with facility of application, evinces neither an inner necessity nor strict consequentiality; and the limitation to the two modes of major and minor, cannot be regarded as positively necessary; or as though amongst the seven tones other positions of the semitone were not possible. If therefore the restoration of the ancient ecclesiastical modes cannot, in respect of our ears, be entertained, still the question arises, whether in fulfilment of the requirements of mankind after further centuries of development, a transformation of the ancient and modern systems, may not lead to results, in which dignified simplicity, and significant vivacity unite, nay, whether a belief in the constant and unrestrainable progress of mankind will not accept this as a certainty.

Plutarch complained long since, in his essay upon music, chapter 17, that the people neglected the enharmonic song; and although a large number of practical men hinder the acceptation of the enharmonic of quarter notes, still it is certain that by means of the same the representation of the most refined expression in simple melodic music would be gained, perhaps without detracting from the decisiveness of harmony. Far too hastily do persons deny the ability of the human ear to comprehend proportions finer than our semitone, for a much greater degree of acuteness falls to the lot of this sense than to any other; and there is no reason for supposing that the perception for euphony was wanting in the ancients. That we can content ourselves with the present system of temperament, the continued existence of our music shows, which would require to be re-arranged in the event of a finer development of the hearing or stricter demands upon purity. Have we not already admitted that the minor semitone (c—c♯) and the augmented fourth (b—e♯) are larger intervals than the major semitone (c—d♭) and the diminished fifth (b—f), and was not the difference of the small comma (c♭—b f♭—e) perceptible to the Greeks? Why may we not with Kretzschmer give ourselves up to the expectation that the independence of the chords of the seventh and ninth will be referred to more positive rules, and instruments and performers be empowered to treat the finer intervals? Already the minor seventh a♭ f d b, which is resolved into *c* minor, ceases to be regarded as equivalent to g♯ f d b, which is resolved into *a* minor.

In all these matters we decide through the capability of the ear, and the feeling of pleasure, which is based upon the cultivation of our collective powers of soul, and which advances through the indefinite to the definite, inasmuch as through the more and more quickened acuteness of consciousness, the number of varieties is reduced and unity is grasped. Still the sense of pleasure is strengthened by the freedom which is often recognisable in the indefinite and vacillating, and we can, therefore, also explain the unpleasantness of canonically pure music from an æsthetical point of view, which we shall take into consideration hereafter.

Art-philosophy rejects much that is possible. Thus the enharmonic genus would undoubtedly be a gain to the characteristic,—but would it also be so to pure formal beauty? This question cannot be answered *à priori*. Equally difficult would it be to explain why the ear cannot pass beyond the number seven, and recognises but impurity in the proportions of 11 and 13. The human organization will, however, have it so. When, finally, with regard to all temperament, mathematical inconclusiveness awakens doubt as to the correctness of theory, the human mind finds satisfaction and enjoyment in that which is unfettered by numbers, and which operates æsthetically in its uncoerced state. Guided by the hand of Nature, the mind advances securely, although not always fortunate in the solution of the problems which arise. The later attempts at explanation, or systematization, as for instance the division of the scale into two trichords, with the semitone attached below the fundamental tone and its octave (c d e—f g a—b c), or the attempted regeneration of the tetrachord system by Kretzschmer, afford proofs of the restlessly progressive understanding, which strives to arrange and enlighten in newly opened provinces.

§ VIII.

HAD the usable thirds been fixed upon, and had chords been discovered and theoretically recognised, Harmony would have resulted. Yet how limited was the extent of this province to the ancients we learn from history. But only those who have not considered that the use of octaves, fifths and fourths, might serve harmonic purposes, have dared wholly to deny their knowledge of harmony. Harmony is the invention of mankind alone,—is his acquired property. The Greeks developed melody to a state of perfection whose powerful effects have been proved, and to an artistic structure no longer comprehensible, and it is hardly possible that that should be entirely wanting with them which forms an important element of human music; for man alone sings and composes in harmonies.

The development of the science was reserved for the days of Christianity, and even then not until ten or eleven centuries had elapsed. The period of rapid progress commenced with the twelfth century, the names of the promoters are lost; two centuries were spent in preparatory labours, during which a very faulty Discant and a rigid counterpoint appeared. To the Netherlanders is due the credit of having, in the 14th century, established a pure harmony, and of having made proper use of the dissonances. But it is not our purpose here to consider the importance and value of harmony, but merely to show that the general arrangement of tones, as a basis for the construction of chords, is a product of human reflection, and that therein the nature of music becomes recognizable.

§ IX.

IN a like manner does the creative spontaneity of the reflecting spirit assert itself *in the determination of rhythmical relations*. Exclusive of the unrhythmical arrangements of sounds in Nature, in which an unity of the diverse parts is wanting, the regular distribution in time of the changing tones appears peculiar to the music of mankind, in which it attains to a legitimate and definite form as musical time. We not only distinguish musical time from free rhythm, in which various divisions of time and of tone mix together in certain relations without forming a well ordered whole, but we also distinguish a coerced time from a free time, and call the former *time* by preference. It makes its appearance in two different stages of musical development, in the earliest and in the latest. In the former it expresses the narrow law of rigid homogeneous forms, where an outer limitation holds the contents together in sharper outline in the latter it brings the freest movement within regular and comprehensible form, without operating restrictively, and it is the property of art. It is therefore wrong to abnegate the evidences of a real art activity which are made apparent by its invention and use.

The uncultivated races, amongst which we find merely beginnings of music, construct their primitive melodies with regard to the vigorous relations of time, —particularly in the accompaniment, in which instruments of rhythm, such as drums and cymbals, are employed. Here then already is Nature subordinated to a law of intelligence, which however operates externally, or as an extra. Whether the time proceeds unequally, as in ancient Bohemian songs, which Dionys Weber communicates in his *School of Ele-*

mentary Music, or whether it continues equal, does not in the main constitute a difference. The divisions do not exist for themselves, as in free rhythm, but the whole is measured up and divided into equal parts, —the external form predominates. But when man attains to intellectual freedom, in which his feelings acquire depth and breadth, and at the same time to the consciousness of a state of legality, the expression of his inner emotional life takes, in music, that definite rhythmical form which we do not call time in the strict sense of the word, but in which we recognise a measurement of time according to rule, in suitable relations.

Therefore, the Grecian music certainly possessed time, but not such as our coerced time, which certain metrists have vainly attempted to foist upon the ancients; for even by the insertion of pauses, no conformity is arrived at. In the varying movement an inner suitability prevailed, but the proportions were not ruled by so strict a conclusion that the contents became bound by a fundamentally maintained equal measurement: on the contrary, in such free time unequal rhythms (for instance ♩ ♪♪♩ ♪♩ ♪♩ ♪♪) were associated with one another. Individual forms, as the dactylic, iambic, anapæstic, approximated to strict legality, still the further development of time was foreign to ancient music. The higher development of the rhythmical element is attained to by art, when it subjects the freest movement to the unity of a firmly sustained equal measurement, and thus, on the one hand, preserves unimpaired the freedom of the condition of activity, and, on the other hand, subjects it to a law of intelligence, and treats it, not only in detail, but as a whole. Then criticism falls to the lot of the more acute reflection, and, as we shall see further on, æsthetical judgment is called into play. Then also human music is perfected. To this state of cultivation it struggled through a slow course of development, for as late as the 12th century, mankind had no knowledge of time proper, but only of the so-called Mensur, in which, however, the three and two part divisions lay concealed. That which was taught with regard to augmentation, diminution, and alteration, by the mensural theory, between this time and the 15th century was arrived at in part by acute combination, although perhaps too artificially; a simpler theory elucidated the procedure in art. The invention of musical time cannot be referred, as Ernst Wagner maintained (*Musikalische Zeitung*, vol. 26, p. 199), to the requirements of the Duet, or to a simple conventional agreement, rather did it of necessity make its appearance in the progress of the development of art, when a definite delineation and characterization was required to associate with the unity of representation. Equally difficult would it be to prove that musical time was first introduced with complete harmony, and was tied to the same. Harmony and its succession existed and exists without a strictly measured time. Again, musical time cannot be accused of hampering the free movement, rather does it sustain the most lively movement in a condition of symmetry, and preserves its comprehensibility: within the limitation of rhythm, the freedom of beauty rules undiminished, and the formless attains to form. But this only becomes possible by selection and separation, and appears essentially effective for æsthetical purposes, inasmuch as it serves for the representation of proportional beauty.

If the rhythm of tones accords with the rythmically moved activity of the feelings, and if therein a spirituality asserts itself in varied emotion, then the power of the intellect rules over it, arranging and moderating, and brings about the creation of an artwork. In this manner the definite effect is produced which music practises by means of time; but time must not be confounded with tempo, as in the frequently quoted narrative of Pythagoras, which philosopher, it is related, endeavoured to calm an intoxicated youth, who, to the music of flutes, endeavoured to set the house of a rival in flames; Pythagoras succeeded in subduing his passions by causing the musicians to play more quietly. Herein, however, we can only recognise the difference between a passionate and a subdued tempo. The full effectiveness of time can only evince itself in modern music, wherein it appears in a state of development.

§ X.

OUR observations here have to do with that which music possesses in fixed rhythmical form and in time. The similar proportion which bar division establishes amongst the divisions of time regarded as a whole, is based upon the simplest numerical arrangements, for only two species of time, the equal and the unequal, or duple and triple, are in use. To these we subordinate equal and unequal divisions; to the latter belong the triplet and the sextuplet. The inner value of the divisions which is not given in the signature, but in the inner structure, and in the manner of performance, so that the smaller notes have a lighter and more lively effect, (the reader will call to mind the so often falsely denoted $\frac{2}{4}$-time, where it should be $\frac{4}{8}$) belongs to the characteristic, while the similarity in the proportions of the regulated tones, which differ in length and brevity, assists in the representation of proportional beauty. But this value has merely relative importance. The semibreve was regarded as a basis, and by its division were obtained the various kinds of time which we express by numbers.

As long as music moved in simple melody like the choral, musical time was given by the melody itself, without the necessity of external determination; but when it became figured and polyphonic in structure, and the progress of the melody more artificial and intricate, a boundary point became requisite, and a sign which, while apparently unimportant, allowed a view of the whole, and rendered it possible to keep a complete orchestra together, and to define an entire performance. Thus human meditation has arranged a complicated affair in the simplest manner, and however unimportant the outer shell may appear, still notation and time signature have in many ways promoted an essentiality. The use of $\frac{2}{16}$ and $\frac{3}{16}$ in ancient times, finds an explanation in the then slower progress of the melodies, and we must not complain if in fugue the minim appears of the value of the crotchet, seeing that the intensive contents, or the forcibly concentrated continuity predominates. The rhythmical law of Arsis and Thesis asserts itself, inasmuch as a strong and a weak division of time is distinguishable, both with respect to extensive character and intensive contents of the tones or notes. With regard to this the doctrines of theorists are mostly at fault, while the praxis grasps that which is correct; for insufficiently is it taught that the strong division on the first beat should be accented, and that the contrary of this constitutes an exception; for hereby the stronger accentuation is confounded with the time contents. From the nature of rhythm proceeds the characteristic which, for instance, allows a distinction between $\frac{12}{8}$ and $\frac{4}{4}$ in triplets, and $\frac{2}{2}$.

§ XI.

THAT which we term initial imperfect bar (Auftakt) seems to be peculiar to the music of mankind. Its explanation has been variously attempted by metrists, inasmuch as we can only recognise the beginning of a rhythm in the strongly accented Arsis,* therefore, some have accounted for it on the supposition of a previous and ideal Arsis, others as a premature onset of power. Only one intelligent being—man alone—makes use of the initial imperfect bar, and it exists in the feelings which find their expression in music. In the feelings the movement or emotion exists before the manifestation thereof, and the outward expression of the same may commence in the middle, and may form part of an unexpressed melody, and be merely that portion of the same which is made prominent.

Thus the Arsis belonging to the Thesis which forms the initial note, may exist in the feelings, and in the presumption of something which preceded it, and is therefore to be regarded as a continuation of a succession already commenced, by which an infinity of the spiritual existence is made known.

* Dr. Hand after the manner of certain metrist, uses the terms Thesis and Arsis in the opposite sense to that universally recognised by musicians.

§ XII.

The recent investigations of Oppelt show that the laws of tone relation are also the laws of rhythm, and that mankind knows but one condition for the two. In rhythm, also, the ear can only calculate within certain limits. The relations of the number 2 give a quieter expression than do rhythms of the number 3, and as with the number 6 consonance ceases, so also the combination of divisions in rhythm. The seven part bar can in itself produce but a disturbing effect, and is not susceptible of free treatment, and the combinations of 11 and 13 are incomprehensible, and sound unpleasant, for the reason that an unity cannot be perceived, nor the contents be arranged and divided. Even in the bar of five divisions four parts are opposed to one, and the Thesis stands in an incongruity with the Arsis, and in the combination of $\frac{2}{4}$ and $\frac{3}{4}$ symmetry is wanting, although it admits of separation into 2 and 3. Therefore roundness and symmetry have been falsely ascribed to this species of time, and that which Seidel advanced to prove that it contains a more beautiful symmetry than is to be found in the number 3, for the reason that in the case of 5 the centre is smaller than the sides, which gives greater variety, was advanced without any regard for accent, or we do not comprehend what in this case the word centre means. To the use by the Greeks of pænoic and cretic measurement no reference need be made, for it is well known that it was but occasionally introduced in comedy, and for comic effects. Amongst the Turks and less cultivated races we certainly observe the use of the bar of five divisions, but we are not equally successful in the discovery of an advanced state of art. Teleman certainly composed several pieces in five part bar, and later attempts of the sort are to be found in the *Musikalische Zeitung*, Vol. xii., 2nd supplement, Vol. xiv., No. 10; but let no one be deceived with respect to these attempts as their authors were.

After the model of Scotch songs, Abeille in his Operetta of *Peter und Aennchen* (vide *Musikalische Zeitung*, 12th year, 3rd supplement) and Boildieu in " La Dame Blanche," have made use of a combination of $\frac{3}{4}$ and $\frac{2}{4}$ time, but the effect is merely delusion, inasmuch as, with regard to Abeille's attempt, of the three preceding quavers the second has the accent so that merely a derangement of $\frac{2}{4}$ time is recognizable. Schultz wrote the song " Hier steh ich unter Gottes Himmel," in $\frac{11}{4}$ time, and intended thereby to raise his hearers above the earth; but the presumptive art work is no less based upon a delusion, inasmuch as deranged ^{2} time is at the bottom of it; for instance, in the first part of the bar two quavers are metamorphosed into two crotchets.

Steuber, the champion of the five part bar (*Musikalische Zeitung*, Vol. xii., p. 116), admits that this species of time is not natural, and is therefore difficult to play; it may, however, with greater reason, be called natural than artistic. Art cannot make use of this time except in cases where the dissonance lends to the pleasing effect, or in *ornamenti* which serve for transition; as the continued rhythm of a whole piece it produces merely an unbearable monotony, and leaves us, as does the dissonance, unsatisfied. Our objection to its employment might certainly result from force of habit, or, as in the case of the five part bar, from a dislike of the extra trouble and attention involved; still that which, in attempts of this kind, displeases us or leaves us unaffected, rests in the forcible extension of the limits laid down for mankind. Immediately beyond this boundary is the five part bar, further removed are those of many divisions which are quite useless. The advertised invention in $\frac{15}{8}$ time can certainly not hope for recognition. The fact that Nature here and there counts and produces in five and seven, creates no ruling principle for human art.

§ XIII.

To mankind rhythm is a well-defined organic structure, capable of receiving the animating contents of melody and harmony. We call that form *organic* in which all particulars are valid in themselves, and which, united, form a Whole, in such a manner, that part to part, and part to the whole stands in well regulated proportion. Such an organism we recognise in the combined rhythmical periods composed of bar groups, in which the separate parts are bounded by segments and cesuræ. The understanding, with deliberation, organises this structure; which as mere calculation would be abstract and dead, if animation were not added, and if an ideality—the Beautiful—did not obtain. But this only occurs in human art. Time, therefore, must not make music rigid, although we must admit that but seldom does performance retain the free movement within limits: while, on the other hand, through neglect of time the melodic proportion is not seldom disturbed, and indeed much more frequently than through deviation in *tempo*.

§ XIV.

A THIRD point for consideration with regard to the peculiar character of intellectual spontaneity in music is *the invention and use of musical instruments*. It is generally taught that instrumental music is not an original product of mankind, but was attained to partly through imitation, partly through its forerunner and creator—vocal music, and that it first makes its appearance amongst the more recent developments of art. Did we desire to make these assertions a matter of dispute, we might with good reason take up the opposite position. It must be admitted that in song we possess an immediate interpretation, which allows no mistake to creep in between the inner emotion and the means of expression; still, between the song and the instrumental performance lies nought but the reflection, which makes a foreign thing its organ, and allows it to take the place of that given by Nature. Therefore, instrumental music is not wanting in originality of invention, and it was given to us immediately with the powers of reflection; consequently, although song may have preceded it, it was not given later than vocal-*music*. Man can never regard his voice otherwise than as an instrument, and he possesses in it the means for the immediate expression of his inner life, as, on the other hand, he lends HIS tone to the manufactured instrument. Even uncultivated races possess musical instruments, and practise them more easily and better than they do song; but it is invariably *man* who possesses them, and who is able to produce tones from things that, in themselves, appear soundless. He, alone, is the creator of musical instruments. He rules over Nature, for he awakens in passive bodies a motion and a life, which serves for a token of his own inner life. The sounds belong to the flute and violin, but the tones into which they are metamorphosed are the tones of the human heart, and not so much are they produced in imitation of the human voice, as they are chosen as its representatives. Self-efficient, mankind progresses and creates—for its own sake—music, which must the more clearly be regarded as an original creation, because it presupposes free reflection, and man does not receive the prepared means immediately from the hand of Nature.

§ XV.

WITH the invention of instruments, art was introduced; while, on the other hand, the development of art led to the improvement and multiplication of instruments. Whether instrumental music was first used to accompany song, or whether the shepherd, as soon as he had discovered the tone of the flute, played without song, cannot be historically determined. Where an artistic application obtains, the instrument first serves for accompaniment, and not until later does this music become independent, and undertake the principal part. We observe a further progression when mankind expresses his inner self by means of many simultaneously sounding voices, and possesses instrumental music of many parts. This was attained to immediately upon the development of harmony in music, and we may take for granted that mutual mediation was the means of securing the whole, for the combination of many voices necessitated a fixed rule of harmony.

§ XVI.

EVERY instrument is the voice of man, and whatever the performer makes audible, whether it be of his own creation, as in improvisation, or in the representation of an art work, it is ever that which exists within himself or within the composer. Therefore, from the instrument of a good performer who does not merely play at random, the soul speaks, and he who simply manipulates his instrument as though it were something foreign, however great his executive ability, ceases to be a musical artist, and becomes himself an instrument, or a machine. When we take into consideration the comparative effects which vocal and instrumental music produce, we shall fail to form a correct judgment, for the reason that song includes the co-operative power of speech, while the music of instruments first becomes perfectly valid in ripened art. Still, the ancient traditions of Orpheus and Amphion are doubtless based upon facts, which bore with them the incontestably powerful effectiveness of instrumental music. Instruments give tone more purely and more correctly than does the natural human voice, and consequently serve as a pattern for the same. Everywhere in this province we observe the free reflection of mankind, and we see this self-energy create, govern, and arrange.

§ XVII.

MUSIC THE IMMEDIATE REPRESENTATION OF THE ACTIVITY OF THE FEELINGS.

THE music of mankind makes itself known, in the second place, as the immediate representation of the activity of the feelings. As being especially important, we must consider this subject acutely and thoroughly, for the results here attained to, form a basis for a collective fundamental view of music, and we obtain a firm foundation for the rules of musical art, and even refine and fix securely, by the removal of heterogeneous demands, the enjoyment of music. From this point we shall be able to mark, more precisely, the boundaries of the province of music, and even to protect it from the disfigurements entailed by the degenerate luxuriousness of sensuous excitement, under which that which is spiritual vanishes, and also to ward off that false claim of the understanding which is here subordinate, even though certain rights may attach to it.

§ XVIII.

MANKIND, as we have seen, sings and creates music, impelled by no blind instinct, which, bound by the corporeal existence, receives external impressions without reacting upon them with spiritual freedom. Not even to the sensations can we attribute the material of music, inasmuch as they only comprehend the sensuous existence, and live only in the outer senses; the animals have them in common with man. In a higher sphere mankind develops the sum of his powers of soul, which, in order to secure unity and a comprehensive survey, we are accustomed to arrange and classify according to the characteristics of their effects. We learn through psychological investigation that the active powers of the soul allow themselves to be distinguished as intellect and feeling, or head and heart; we know that the activity of the disposition appears as emotion and longing or inclination, and we learn from the science of psychology in what manner, and according to which laws of Nature, the emotions become affections, the inclinations develop into passions. Thus, in order to comprehend the conditions of soul which lie at the bottom of these phenomena, we are referred back to the simplest activity of the feelings, and recognise therein the foundation of musical representation. If, in the science of psychology, all were agreed with respect to that which we term feeling, there would be no necessity for further discussion, and adhering to the, in other respects, determinative usages of language, we might rely upon an equally certain comprehension as when we speak of the fantasy, and of the understanding. But the case is otherwise. Even now the *literati* and investigators have not been able to agree in the comprehension of the idea, and nowhere does such a confusion of language prevail as where the feeling is in question, for sometimes the independence of this faculty of the soul is denied; sometimes feeling is confounded with other activities of the soul. Therefore we cannot be exempted from a general investigation, but we will first stipulate that, in speaking of various faculties of the soul, only various manifestations and activities of the one faculty thereof, only various forms of manifestation shall be understood.

§ XIX.

FEELING is not representation, with which it is often confounded or identified, for representation has to do with the unity of an objective diversity; feeling is itself subjective unity, and exists, considered for itself, without representation, and before or after the same, and one and the same representation can excite quite opposite feelings. Feeling is, further, not judgment, not even the immediate manifestation of critical powers of thought, indeed, rather do idea and reflection dissipate feeling or weaken it, as in the case of criticism applied to art works; and even when an union of the two takes place, and we observe a reflection of feeling, feeling must be distinguished from sensation, or from the potency of sensuous pleasure, for this confines itself to comprehension through the instrumentality of the senses, and has to do with an external. They are more nearly related, for sensuous and spiritual existence melt into one another, and if in the contemplation of music we find ourselves at the same time referred to the sensations, and if, for the realization of the effect of music, healthy organs of hearing are necessary, and, further, if the production in this respect is essentially determined by the condition of the sensuous comprehension, we rightly keep the two spheres separate from one another in order that we may be able to point out, in the province of intellectual self-energy, the peculiar nature of music.

Feeling is the faculty by which man, immediately and without ideas, inwardly grasps the spiritual existence, and inasmuch as the external becomes internal, the alien becomes peculiar, so that which is presented lives spiritually. We feel within us all that which affects us or is otherwise presented, as being our own spiritual condition, we feel immediately that which is presented to us, whether it belongs to earthly conditions or is derived from the world of ideas, and we feel ever a spirituality, and therefore also the sensuous in its spiritual import. Feeling also comprehends within it the contemplative existence of the spirit, and as all spiritual life is subordinate to an idea and is governed by the same, feeling consequently falls under the idea of the Beautiful, opposite to the ideas of the True and Good, to which the provinces of the understanding, and of the endeavour, or the will, belong. We define this contemplative soul life as being æsthetic, inasmuch as an immediate consciousness and comprehension takes place. The True and the Good are also felt, but always æsthetically, that is when they are presented to us as something which can be immediately comprehended, and which is not merely representation: consequently it not seldom occurs that the True and Good are called Beautiful in ordinary language. What I feel, I feel under and according to the fundamental idea of the Beautiful, just as all thought takes place under and according to the idea of the Truth. Hereby, however, is not said that all that I feel is beautiful; but in all that which is felt, something immediately comprehensible is contained which constitutes the primary foundation of the Beautiful; and we directly comprehend the spiritual existence, and in a manner that is foreign to the understanding; the form of appearance of the spiritual is the Beautiful, which becomes prominent in Nature, in Art, and in the beautiful Soul. But we cannot regard feeling as the mere humour of good or bad health, or of pleasure and displeasure; rather does energy exist within it, for I feel something inasmuch as I become immediately conscious of it and possess it as my existence. Feeling melts with desire and passes into affection, and a feeling lies at the bottom of every desire and passion. But both feeling and affection constitute the power of the spirit, which, by reason of this relationship, can be regarded as a whole. In it unite the ideas of the Beautiful and the Good, and the pleasingly Beautiful becomes valuable, wins our affections, and is desired and appropriated. As long as love consists of pure feeling it has but Beauty for its object, and confines itself to the contemplation of the same; as affection it strives after something valuable and gratifying and makes demands upon enjoyment.

§ XX.

THIS activity of the feelings stands in collateral relationship with the activity of thought, and without being abruptly separated from it (for nothing exists separate in the soul of man, and we cannot by means of words and ideas divide the Whole of the Spirit into chambers) forms an antithesis. Contemplation, and reflection, and feeling, act and re-act upon one another, and mutually exchange places; still they are distinct energies which predominantly restrain and supplant one another, therefore we may assign to their effectiveness certain peculiar provinces. By many persons, feeling is regarded as being little more than a negation of the understanding, and the restricted man of understanding cannot perceive anything more therein than obscure representations and unclear ideas; there is nevertheless a spiritual life, and a world without ideas, which cannot be rendered comprehensible by general representation, and of which we become clearly conscious in the moments which raise us above the visible world. He who has felt his heart—moved by an invisibility—beat more strongly in joy and in sorrow, in the contemplation of the Beautiful, in the ecstasy of love, or in the elevation of devotion, bears the evidence within him; he merely feels; and thoughts which preceded are not present,—not even a thought of himself. Consequently language fails him, and he describes that which lives within him as unutterable. From this fact springs the by-no-means slight difficulty of an explanation, inasmuch as in order to be able merely to speak thereof, we must subordinate the feeling to an idea. Language, in such cases, has recourse to analogies or to allegorical representations, similarly as in matters appertaining to music we speak of thoughts which are not thoughts.

§ XXI.

As the outer senses of the eye and ear immediately comprehend sensuous impressions and contact, and previous to all reflection the existence of the phenomenon is thus determined, so the inner sense of the soul comprehends its own spiritual existence, and with it, not only that which addresses itself to the soul and affects it, but also that which is intuitive. He who feels, stands, therefore, in immediate relation with a spiritual world, with the insensuous, which also lies at the root of sensuous phenomena, with the Pure and Holy and with God. He lives the life, and is as certain thereof as of his life. That from which the ideas of thought develop themselves, described by philosophers as an *à priori*,—and which constitutes a primary possession of the soul, creates feeling directly from the source of inner contemplation. All investigation in the province of Truth, ends ascending in the ultimate unqualified recognition of the Truth. Elevation, animation, joy, limitation, pain and other denominations, serve the more closely to define the nature of the activity of the soul. But we shall carefully avoid the system by which psychologists refer all feelings to the heads of pleasure and displeasure; they are unable to interpret those feelings in which neither that which is really pleasant nor unpleasant is to be found, and which, nevertheless, exist, from the fact that, setting aside pleasure or pain, they immediately and without ideas become conscious of an existence. Thus we feel Truth and Consonance for themselves, and only afterwards can that which is pleasing in them come under consideration, when that which is True accords with our spiritual requirement and satisfies it.

§ XXII.

THE activity of the feelings is in reality life, whose form is made known in inner emotion. Excited by sensuous impressions or moved by ideal objects, feeling busies itself, and grasps in Nature and human life, in the real and ideal, the spiritual which is related to it. Therefore to the term *emotion* of *feeling*, to which custom lends special significance, we may ascribe a broader meaning. This motion of the inner life appears in visible form, spacially in the expression of the mien and the motion of the body, or in mimicry; temporally through tones in music. Tones are in themselves moved life, and become the expression of an inwardly moved existence. Representation and idea choose the words of language for their tokens, but where the feeling attains to expression without further mediation, musical sounds serve it, as we may perceive in the interjections; or language and tone become one, as in song. Rousseau, therefore, rightly asserted, although his words have been misunderstood, that music speaks the language which is spoken by the child at its mother's breast, before it understands words.

This explanation of the expression of the feelings by means of tones, leads us securely to the recognition of the condition and boundaries of music. As life is immediately comprehended by the feelings, so also music immediately makes manifest the feelings without the help of any other means,—we recognize feeling as having become sound. But here, perhaps, it will be remarked that not all music can be regarded as the language of the feelings, for often it is rather a mere play of tones. How this play of tones may occur will hereafter appear; but it remains undeniable that purely human music (and not all can be regarded as such) always emanates from the spirit as the innermost sphere of life, and is the manifestation of life itself, whether it be through the human voice, or through the instrument which supplies its place. In both self-energy obtains, and the tones drawn from, and lent to the voiceless object, are the tones of mankind. The breath of man lends animation to the rigid, but musically capable wood of the flute, and that which he corporeally breathes into it is spiritual emotion, as those kinds of tones in which spiritual life is easily recognized, must be considered the most perfect.

§ XXIII.

BUT when the activity of the feeling thus finds its expression in music, and an inner impulse forces the soul to this expression, we might naturally expect, whenever feeling is called into activity, to hear only song and music, which is not, and cannot be always the case. In the removal of this difficulty, we must take two points into consideration. Feeling itself becomes a tone-picture which the imagination is able firmly to retain, although no communication may follow, nor any expression by means of the sounds of the voice appear necessary. In the same manner that we think in words, and consequently exercise in thought a soundless inner language, so also the feeling moves in tones which are not audible. He who is joyful not seldom sings and makes music within himself, without being heard, to a greater extent than the world around him may surmise; and men who cannot sing a single interval correctly, or play any instrument, sometimes bear the music within them, and live in it more than many a musician; indeed the real tone poet or composer works for the most part within himself, without touching an instrument. Therefore we are fain to contradict the opinion advanced by certain writers, amongst them Gottfried Weber (*Cæcilia*, Vol. i., p. 325), to the effect that music owes its origin, not to the feelings, but to the ear; and that, in the first place, the receptive power of the sense of hearing must have been aroused to the beauty of tones before the relationship of the heart and the ear could become effective. The emotion of the inner life is the earliest.

The second point for consideration lies in the fact that we seldom preserve the activity of the feelings in a perfectly pure state, but allow the reflection to step in between very rapidly. The understanding then changes all that which is within us into ideas and words. But music distinguishes itself from language by its exemption from intervening causes, and by the natural expression through which feeling void of ideas is portrayed. The greater part of language is based upon conventional use and arbitrary selection. When speaking man complains of the insufficiency of word description, and of the poverty of language, or even acknowledges that the object cannot be expressed in words, it still remains possible to the tones of music, to grasp immediately that which is felt, and to make it perceptible. Thereby no small degree of decisiveness falls to its share, but the rule for its measurement must not be a logical one. Where the idea is not sufficient, where no picture can be given to the eye, music takes up the resigned function of representation, and is more successful than any other artistic means.

Shortsighted was the judgment of those who asserted that the task of music is to imitate language.

§ XXIV.

FROM that which we have already stated, the sphere and boundaries of music may be determined. It represents feeling, but not the objective matters of feeling, and asserts, throughout, its subjective character. Everything external must, for it, become internal, which, however, cannot occur in all cases. However much the common understanding may require it, music cannot and will not represent visible objects of Nature, thoughts and ideas. The formative arts and painting select the objects of Nature and their diverse appearances, that in their representation they may lay down the ideas of Beauty and Perfection. Music, in and external to Art, gives only feelings and inner emotions—without signs that may be immediately associated with an idea, and not imitatively, whereby comparison may be made with an original. The painter and the sculptor speak like the poet, comprehensibly, in a previously formed language, which another may readily follow, while music brings its own language, and, in its individual validity, lays no claim to general understanding. That all this, notwithstanding it may be recognised and appropriated, is provided for by the power given to the human heart, and indeed with nearer relationship than is given to the head. And if the ultimate aim of the poet and the painter be to speak to the heart, and affect it, this is the first aim of music, and its most important tendency. Limited to the innermost activity of the soul, it possesses a greater abundance therein than the outer world can offer, and if in the feelings no juxtaposition is to be found, and no objective difference allows us to distinguish between the subjects, still, in the succession of emotions and activities, lies an infinity which is capable of a thousandfold relations to the High and Highest, and secures immediate gratification in an assured unity. Men have sung and made music in all times, but when the Christian religion aroused life into feeling, and filled it with the highest ideal of existence, humanity could find in tones only, a sufficient means of expression, and a new art, as a Christian art was attained to.

§ XXV.

WE must not overlook the relation which exists between thought and feeling—which appears as a disparity—if we wish to be successful in answering a series of questions which have a decided bearing upon the knowledge of the nature of music. Firstly, we may ask, When is thought representable in music? Only when it is not mere thought, but has become active inner existence, when it does not appear before the soul as an object, but has entered into life itself. Many have fallen into the error of regarding man as a being that observes and thinks in ideas, without recognizing his participation in the creation of a spiritual world. Still, thought and idea have also a reality, and this becomes life in us, inasmuch as we transform thought into our spiritual existence. Therein the truth of the sensuous world, and also the eternal idea of faith, becomes our positive possession; and that which thus constitutes our inner life,—thought transformed into feelings—we utter in moved tones, as the moved life of the soul.

Therefore music without words is the purest and the most primitive, and not only as regards instrumental music, but also as regards song; for collective Nature sings and sounds without words. Its productions soar most freely in their own flight.

Kant erroneously regarded it as the vehicle of poetry; but it by no means evinces more inner import when combined with words, but simply becomes more comprehensible, and attains to greater perspicuity, and readily admits of judgment. Thus Haydn treated the music in the songs of the "Seven words of our Saviour," thus Vierey, Schmidt, and others adapted suitable texts to some of the pianoforte compositions of Beethoven, as did Heinrich Schütz to the "Sehnsuchts Walzer," and Mendelssohn composed songs without text. But we daily hear bitter complaints of such singers as do not pronounce the text distinctly, and we are expected to regard the words as the chief thing. We should not consider that which is good to be absolutely the best, but make nicer distinctions.

Where understanding and perception are associated, as in the Romance, or the action of an Opera, we have, before all, a necessity for the text; but where, on the other hand, pure feeling is represented—as, for instance, the delight in awakened Nature, or melancholy, —tone and its symbolic power are sufficient, and we require nothing more than the purely musical. Nothing occurs more often than that a scene or action of life is adopted as a text for a musical work, whereby feeling is translated into idea. But we soon observe the insufficiency, for instance, in the Overture of

Beethoven, Op. 115, wherein some persons imagine to hear, in the diverging parts, a war of words that gradually becomes louder, in which the speakers move into opposition, but which at length passes into subdued murmurs and jeers, and resolves itself into the most perfect unity. This would be the musical representation of a constitutional assembly, which could only be derisively represented in music. Similarly our judgment must have regard for circumstances, when we are inclined to take offence at the insufficiency of all narrations concerning music, or in the criticism of musical works. The language of the understanding cannot suffice, and the assistance which we receive from typical representation is not satisfactory, for the reason that its comprehension pre-supposes an agreement as to the validity of the figures used; but we cannot justify the style of the musical daily papers, which continually speak of the Incomprehensible, and, in vague and empty phrases, largely puffed out with allegories, express nothing. The necessity for a thorough work on Æsthetics becomes more apparent in the fact that we have not yet attained to a fixed musical terminology. Demonstration will never suffice, as we observe in the sphere of sensuous perception, where we cannot positively describe in what manner blue and red differ from one another, or how it is that certain things have a pleasant taste or smell. With this fact before us, we shall considerately avoid blaming those, who, on hearing music, comprise various effects under the general denomination of beautiful, or excellent, and, unconcerned as to the finer distinctions, satisfy themselves with the general effect; or who describe as *high* that which others call *deep*. The activity of the understanding also affects the spirit, when it brings about conditions, and we can portray musically, the vacillation of the soul in doubt, its absorption and meditation, the inner strife of the will, &c., &c., but hereby we ever remain within the sphere of subjective life-relations. Here we may estimate the value of the assertion as to the apparently meaningless character of music, which led Nägeli to deny that music had any contents, and that the more meaningless it is, the more excellent does it become. Such is music merely to the understanding, to which indeed it does not immediately offer a contents.

§ XXVI.

THE agitations of desire, affection, and passion have their origin in the feelings, and although they may supplant and weaken, or even entirely remove pure feeling, still the coveted object must first be presented to the feelings in order to be striven after, or avoided as pleasant or unpleasant. Therefore they also fall within the province of musical representation. That which, in desire and affection, constitutes the state of activity, that effort to appropriate and struggle to obtain the desired good, becomes audible as a surging and striving, as a changing and blending of the feelings in tones. Still even here the object of the passion or affection cannot be described, and we cannot comprehend what the wished-for good may be, but merely the condition of soul excited and maintained by the same. This distinguishes itself characteristically according to the nature of the desire, of which a particular feeling always forms the basis; and love, revenge, and jealousy, express themselves differently. All that which is added in ideas by the understanding is borrowed and foreign.

§ XXVII.

No one will deny to feeling the legality which is unconditionally admitted with regard to thought. The laws which Nature has laid down for the feelings, apply also to music, inasmuch as the representation should and does accord with the contents which are to be represented. Every feeling and every condition of the spirit has in itself, and also in music, its particular tone and rhythm, just as every idea has its particular word. This modifies the musical representation generally. But hereby the expression of art does not come under consideration, but only the law of Nature by which the manifestation accords with that which is within us. Not only do the vehement and soft, the strong and weak, find in high and clear, deep and dull tones, their suitable expression; but this is also the case with the particular conditions and activities of the spirit. Therefore hope, despair, fear, the blessing of faith, and love, possess their peculiar expression in tone and rhythm, even although this tone and rhythm cannot be theoretically assigned. In Romberg's music to Schiller's "Glocke" not only the idea or words "and hopes" demanded the high open tone, but this was required also by the feeling.

Psychology in its course of observation describes, successively, the various kinds of feeling, and divides them into pleasure and displeasure, joy and grief, traces their development to the highest degree of the affection, and points out the transitions into endeavours and passions. With respect to the limiting feelings, a great diversity and a great number of gradations are offered, between displeasure and dejection, through all grades of sorrow and sadness, to depressing melancholy and acute grief. The province of pleasure comprehends all gradations from lightly moved joy, through the more or less free emotion of gaiety, to dithryambic wildness. Thereto attach themselves the feelings of power, courage, and daring. The feelings of love and hate, from the first emotion of awakening inclination and longing, to passionate impetuosity, and the revel in enjoyment, comprehend the richest province, and thousandfold modifications.

It is however difficult for philosophy to separate, and describe exactly, each particular condition, and still more difficult is a theoretical semiotic of music. For the most part, the chief heads, only, can be determined, in illustration of the rules; the particulars are left to Nature, which, if undisturbed by foreign admixture, always strikes its mark. Of the passions, those generally cannot attain to musical representation which are associated with particular reflections, as, for instance, greed and veneration, while the more general pride and arrogance, find more easily their expression.

On regarding that which we have hitherto advanced, it would appear that the so-oft-repeated assertion as to the indefiniteness of the feelings, has not been taken into consideration. When, however, considered more closely it will appear that merely a misunderstanding obtains. The indefiniteness exists only in the understanding, inasmuch as it is not possible to the same to subordinate the particulars to ideas, or to treat all signs as logical. Therefore that which bears within it its own peculiar definiteness, appears, to the understanding, to be indefinite, and this recognises an unutterable condition of the feelings. The indefiniteness of the feelings stands thus in an inverse relation to comprehensibleness, and, for this reason, many persons have denied to music the power of representing definite feelings, and Hoffmann accredited it merely with the expression of unutterable longing. Such an opinion every good musical work will refute, for therein neither tone nor rhythm can be changed.

Truly it is impossible to perceive in Beethoven's Funeral March whether a father mourns his children, or a lover his mistress, still, unmistakably is expressed therein the grief of life, in which such differences of outer relations vanish, but the heart is quite certain of its grief. Beyond the earth, that is beyond the sphere of ideas and of sensuousness, the love of the child and the love of the enamoured are but one, and do not appear different through finite circumstances. The object which has excited the feeling, and to which the latter is directed, does not attain to nearer definition, but the feeling is in itself the more definite.

Truly those who have condemned the modern nomenclature of musical works, such as "Farewell to London," "Recollections of St. Petersburg," &c., have sufficient grounds; but with the justifiable rejection of all empty terms, the fact of giving names to the expression of particular feelings, must not also be forbidden. We shall see further on, within what limits this practice becomes perfectly justifiable.

We can ascribe to music a much greater degree of definiteness of representation than falls to the lot of any other art, for it is not only impossible to the painter, to represent feelings in so definite a manner, —paintings offering but a trace of the same,—but even the mimic exhibitor cannot, by means of expression, speak to the heart as it is possible to do so by means of tones.

§ XXVIII.

THE nature of feeling asserts itself no less in rhythm than in melody. Feelings are inner excitements in time which pass more or less quickly and which are uniform, or of changing form. Therefore they contain a rhythm within themselves. Music immediately grasps this inner rhythmical life, and represents it in her forms, without being prejudiced by reason of the fact, that thought often finds something indefinite therein. In this activity of the inner elements of life, a law of continuity (Stetigkeit) obtains, and we can observe therein a beginning, growth, decline, and transition; the feelings pass into one another, are never broken by a leap; this could only occur through the accidental operation of an external. Graduality is the form of its growth and the related attaches itself to the related; where antitheses meet together, the influence of contrast acts mediatingly. Therefore every change occurs in accordance with the laws of connection, similarly as this takes place in the association of pictures and representations. Everywhere appears diversity united by an inner coherence; and unity which has its origin in the soul's entirety.

And thus it is with music also which is not absolved from the laws of continuity, for it exists in a state of coherence, in constant change, in decline, in rising and falling. A mere aggregation of diverse representations of feeling does not constitute music, and even when antitheses occur, or in *baroque* contrast appear as a disparity, still the hypothesis of continuity is not destroyed. The reason why much in our existing music displeases or embarrasses us lies partly in the neglect of this law of continuity.

§ XXIX.

THE province of music is immediate time present, for even as I feel when affected by an influential existence, and grasp the same, inasmuch as it becomes my own, so also I represent. The past, then, can only be treated as the present, and every historical relation vanishes. By this presentiality is explained, on the one hand, the great power which music has asserted at all times. It proceeds and operates with a certainty unknown to any other art, for that which exists within it also penetrates immediately, as the nearest Present, into the spirit of the hearer, without ambiguity and without illusion. It excites similarity of feeling, without standing in need of explanation by language, and the hearts of men being nearer allied than their heads, this coincidence is thereby much more readily brought about. Through this presentiality music speaks more forcibly to the heart; and more lasting is the pleasure, for a frequent repetition does not so readily fatigue, or render indifferent, as it does in the case of productions of the art of painting, or even of poetry. On the other hand, the province in which musical art operates is limited, for it cannot treat of the past in its remoteness, nor represent that which is foreign to it in an objective picture,

For music everything external must become internal.

§ XXX.

But not alone is the world of the finite, and of the sensuous, given to the feelings; the contemplative activity of the soul, touches and grasps also a higher world. How it is that our spiritual existence is filled and moved by that which is presented to the contemplation, is readily explained, and every one knows how joy and serenity, sadness and grief, despair and hope, excited by that which we have experienced, raise and stir, check and depress our spiritual powers; how therein alien nature blends with our own and becomes our own. Still, how feeling may receive within it something general or ideal, and how music may represent the same, does not become clear to every one in the daily experiences of life. There is, however, an ideal feeling which originates in a higher province than that of the ideas, and which allows man to pass into immediate contact with a world which is not attained to by the ideas, for he thinks the eternal and infinite in ideas, and feels it as his life in ideas. From all that is finite and conditional, the spirit of the Unconditional, the Eternal Truth, the Infinite Freedom, the Godhead speaks to his heart, and as this spirit becomes one with his own spirit, and he bears it within him, and is penetrated, raised, and blessed by it, this constitutes the contents of his feeling which then expresses itself in tones. Thus music truly cannot represent ideas themselves, but it attests the existence of the idea within us, and excites it, raises us above the finite, and secures to us the participation in a life which operates beyond and above the limitations of Space and Time. That which, in majestic and beautiful music, affects our profounder soul, we term unutterable and indefinable. It is the Infinite itself which receives us, and which we bear within us. In this elevation above all earthly things, into a region wherein words are no longer sufficient, a magic peculiar to music operates. It makes us free, and tears us from the limits which ideas draw around us: the spirit then feels itself freed from the conditions of a poor earthly existence. Therefore it also makes man happy, and he can speak of it as a blessing, although the cold worldly man of understanding may smile at it, or he who is enchained by mere sensuous enjoyment, may regard it as empty and void.

On listening to a performance of Mozart's Zauberflöte—however trivial may be the import of the—in part—tasteless text—he who grasps the music purely and deeply, and gives himself up, unprejudiced, to that which is ideal in the same, will find in the end that nothing further remains than that state of blessedness which culminates in a desire to be removed entirely from everything worldly. This is regarded by many as mere enthusiasm, and that which is rightly regarded as the language of longing, and as a manifestation of the Insensuous, they call the expression of obscure feelings. But they are the clearest and brightest contemplations in which we become conscious of our God, of our future freedom and blessedness. The formative arts give body to ideas, and strive thus to humanize the Divine; but music, on the contrary, seeks to change the Sensuous into the Spiritual, and to transform the Human into the Divine: therein it is assisted by the finest and an invisible material, with which it creates ethereal forms, that no eye may perceive, but which the soul, as it were, exhales; it resolves the Spacial into Temporal, the Passive into Activity, and leads to ideal life and freedom, in which finer spirits are given over to the enjoyment of Infinity. But even grief leads us thereto. We should not find pleasure in sad and pathetic music, if, besides the limiting impression, it did not represent the Infinite, and waken an idea of faith in eternal love, and the victory of spiritual freedom. In the activity of the spirit there are central points from which music proceeds in the purest, greatest abundance, and, being heard, penetrates the most deeply and excites the most powerfully. These are Religion, and Love in its diverse forms.

§ XXXI.

NOTWITHSTANDING the extensive compass of this effectiveness, and the great importance of the music of mankind, many persons have raised complaints as to the poverty of the same, and have imagined to discover a prop to its worth in its association with poetry. Music, they say, lacks the means of awakening a complete picture in the soul of the listener, and can only represent ideas in general, and reproduce a general effect (*vide* "Greipenkerl's Æsthetik," page 371). Such complaints may be reasonable, if, in the activity of the soul, nothing further than representation exists. This we may certainly find sufficient for this life, but beyond it we shall not endure with ideas of the understanding, and even with our present existence a purer and loftier foreknowledge is associated. He who demands merely prosaic thought, moves here, undoubtedly, in a foreign province. Not in the imitation of representations does music busy itself (in vain would it attempt the same), but that which it offers in great riches, unites that which is general and particular, and includes that which is significant. We do not wish to perceive individual things, which, for the most part, fall to the lot of sensuous contemplation, nor does the real listener to music seek for a translation into ideas; but clearly and completely the individual feeling addresses the soul as an universality, and at the same time preserves its ideal character. The power of thought may appear rich when it combines, in one derived picture, the thousandfold diversities to unities; but still feeling, and therefore music cannot be termed poor, because the former immediately comprehends life without a picture, and the latter immediately makes life known in similar emotion. If we survey, without prejudice, the province of music, we shall observe that which is the greatest and most comprehensive therein. Everything high and low which a condition of soul is capable of producing lies within it.

§ XXXII.

WE have already referred to Nägeli's opinion which denies a meaning to music. He added that it only offers form, a combination of tones, and successions of tones according to rule. That which is true in this assertion shall be considered hereafter, but at present only that which is untrue will occupy our attention. Without expression of an intellectual contents, music ceases to be human and beautiful. We cannot therefore imagine it as mere empty form, nor place it on an equality with the song of birds. What it is that constitutes empty music we shall elsewhere have opportunity of observing, but, in itself, it cannot be called a mere play of form. The world which is present to mankind, penetrates into the spirit, and returns from thence again to the visible forms. The form of my inner existence is my existence itself. All thought and will, all participation in a spiritual existence, and the reception of the supersensuous, becomes a condition of the soul, which the understanding can again denote in abstract pictures; all this the feeling immediately grasps, and with the external activity of life, which accords with the inner emotion, represents every condition in its own peculiar manner. This is not mere form, but life expresses itself in life, and he who then requires more than tone and rhythm may be compared with a person who denies meaning to a painting because the characters in the picture do not move and speak, and the bubbling springs do not murmur. Truly we cannot expect objective representations in music, but only inner conditions of life, and even these not in abstractions, but in immediate appearance, and for direct transmission into other souls. The excited and moved life of him who sings and produces music, propagates itself, exciting and moving, into the soul of the listener, and a more intimate conformity and blending is not possible. A misunderstanding cannot occur, and soul penetrates into soul. But we err (again we repeat it) when our demand for contents is only directed to ideas. The Allegro of a Symphony has been interpreted as the destiny of a man who enjoys life, who sits among his children, or who actively passes to and fro in life's market; the Adagio as the anxiety of a maiden who has not for a long time received a letter from her beloved. Music cannot and will not give such meanings for representations, and he who takes upon himself the right of demanding the same, need not be angry when others banter him with creations of the imagination, and, for instance, point out in Mendelssohn's Overture to the Midsummernight's Dream, the particular bar at which the moonlight appears, and the elfs dance.

§ XXXIII.

As the representation of the activity of the feelings, music cannot take up that which is passive and rigid, for in the activity of the human soul a continuous series of emotions is contained, in which diversity develops itself throughout time, inasmuch as to a particular fundamental feeling, related emotions attach themselves, near or remote transitions transpose into new conditions, and the degrees of activity are now heightened, and now diminished. Relation and contrast operate together to form combinations, and not seldom unite that which appears quite heterogeneous, Thus music chooses tone and rhythm, and *tempo* for both, and with them it passes through time and bounds into life. Before a picture the spectator stands silent, and buries himself in the same, while that which is lasting in music, such as sustained tones and chords, is disquieting and may become burdensome to the spirit. But this manner of seizing upon one and bearing one along with it, which is characteristic of music, has the effect of making the soul free from all that is foreign, of lightly removing from the soul all that which disturbs and checks it, and by the freedom of its flight of also securing the delight which free spirits enjoy. Herein lies the healing and strengthening power of music, which is far too little regarded by those sanative artists, who do not merely restore the body by means of that which is corporeal, that we are able to speak of any decided results. And yet a proper use of this means would doubtless lead to satisfactory effects. Of the great influence of music in creating a friendly disposition, and in calming or appeasing the excited or exasperated, we are in possession of many memorable facts. Laborde, in his "Essai sur la Musique" relates the following anecdote of Alessandro Stradella, a master of the violin in the middle of the seventeenth century. While staying in Venice he won by his music the heart of Hortensia, a Roman lady, who sped with him back to Rome. Her guardian, enraged at this abduction, persuaded a young man, whose destined bride she was, to revenge the insult with the blood of the seducer. The bridegroom hastened to Rome. He ascertained that Stradella would perform in a certain church, and betook himself there, with a dagger concealed beneath his cloak. From Stradella's performance spoke love, heavenly love, and the jealous lover's desire for revenge was pacified, so that he wrote back to Venice to say that he arrived too late, and that Stradella had already flown, and he even went so far as to offer Stradella the means of escaping the attempts at revenge. Of an artist of the name of Palma, who lived in Naples, in the middle of the seventeenth century, Martinelli, in his critical letters, relates the following story:—An usurer, to whom Palma was indebted for a considerable sum of money, came roughly into his house to cause him to be arrested

Instead of making answer to the insulting remarks levelled at him, Palma sang with hoarse voice an Ariette. On perceiving that the old miser became interested, he sat himself down at the pianoforte, and sang a second Aria, with accompaniment. He observed that certain chords produced a great effect upon his creditor, and his efforts, in the end, were so successful that the usurer no longer made demands for payment, but on being asked by Palma for a further loan, granted him the same. Upon gems, the ancients represented Amor, riding on the back of a lion, and playing the lyre,—a thoughtful allegory of the power of music.

§ XXXIV.

MUSIC THE PRODUCT OF THE SPIRITUALITY AND OF THE TOTALITY OF THE POWERS OF THE MIND.

WE have hitherto described the nature of music as the representation of the feelings, and have justified its subjective character, inasmuch as we have separated it from the world of ideas. This is the natural music of man, who, however, when operating intellectually and freely, is active with his whole soul, and, in advanced development, makes demands for the complete gratification of the spirit. As the mere representation of the feelings, music would not therefore completely unite within itself the spiritual interests and consequently would not gratify them. We should indeed secure in it, and through it, an elevation above the confines of the Sensuous, convert the sensations into feelings, and become conscious of a participation in an ideal world, but all this would readily lose itself in the Irregular and Indefinite, and the connection in which our spiritual existence stands with the objective world would be lost to us. But in the feelings, there is but subjective definiteness, and still the demand of our spiritual life is for an objective certainty. We ever strive to attain to this, and a product can only gratify both the creative and contemplative spirit, when it makes demands upon the whole being of the soul. An object which the soul feels, and thinks, and contemplates, and which thus calls all powers equally into activity, allows us to become certain of our spiritual freedom. We cannot and will not be mere creatures of feeling, and every predominating disposition becomes a disagreeable partiality. But this does not occur in music when it addresses itself to art cultivation, for then the unity of the employed powers of the soul is associated with it, inasmuch as feeling and reflection penetrate one another, and the power of the imagination, as the property of the picture and of the comprehensible representation, is called into play.

To define this third character, a word is wanting; but as we use the word Spirit to describe that power of the soul which is opposed to feeling, we will here make use of the term Spirituality or Totality. The collective spiritual powers immediately become active when music-practising man touches the province of art, or even only approaches it. Then, man not only feels and hears, but he also thinks and contemplates ideas, and creates pictures of the fantasy. Were music only a representation of the feelings and that which is associated therewith, were it only an accidental association, then Kant would have had right on his side, when he asserted that in the province of reason, but little value attaches to it. Still, that which exists in the feelings, and which, being grasped by the same, attains to musical representation, acquires through the concurring participation of the understanding or the reflection, and the power of the imagination, even the possibility of representation, order, comprehensibleness, and objective importance, and—through the participation of reason—a clear subordination of ideas. Through this co-operation music becomes universal in character, and it becomes an art. But it is the intellect which lays open the ideal world to the feelings, and which converts that which it grasps into thoughts and contemplations, which subjects the representation to rule, and which, consequently, when the inner life attains to expression, exerts its ruling power in the creation of a musical art work—tones and movements being decided upon by the spontaneous reflection—with the same degree of activity which it evinces in the comprehension of the same.

§ XXXV.

In enquiries concerning the nature of music, as in psychological investigation generally, the abrupt division of the faculties of the soul will not suffice; we are therefore led to recognise many separate points in the collective effect of these powers which never exist in a divided state. Still, at the onset, it appears necessary to point out the relation in which these faculties stand to one another. The understanding stands partly in antithesis, partly in alternating relation to the feelings; but we must here guard against a common error, by which we assume antithesis where only an increased activity gains the ascendancy, as similarly, the assumption that feeling is circumscribed and weakened by thought, is mostly based upon the fact, that the soul, which gives itself up entirely to meditation, cannot at the same time lend its power to feeling. We shall, further on, find a confirmation of this in the rules for composition. On the other hand, that which, at the same time, employs the understanding, can enhance the activity in a condition of feeling, similarly as the connoisseur of music hears more than the dilettante, inasmuch as he, at the same time, sets his understanding in activity, although, perhaps, without preserving a so powerful or pure state of feeling. Through reflection, feeling gains in extension, although, perhaps, at the cost of intensive strength. The feeling becomes the image of the fantasy, and thereby, on the one hand, gains, not only by becoming more comprehensible, but also by acquiring enhanced vivacity, form, and colour; on the other hand, it readily loses itself in forms, and levels the general import. This finds in no instance more positive proof than in musical productions. The vivacity of the feelings is enhanced, and enduringly maintained, if the fantasy associates a richer sum of images, and thus not only engages the soul through diverse interests, but awakens new feelings, which unite with the original feelings, and strive with them for the ascendancy, and perhaps supersede them. The clarity of the powers of imagination is associated herewith to advantage, for the reason that a clearly defined picture is well adapted to receive the truth of life, and the magic of beauty, and with these speaks to the heart, in such a manner that no misunderstanding, still less indifference, can result.

§ XXXVI.

THE collective efficiency of our powers of soul, which react upon one another, and the spiritual character of music are made known (1) in Melody and Harmony; (2) in the free play of musical pictures; (3) in the modification of expression; (4) in the subordination to the idea of Beauty. Herein the entire nature of music, in all its elements, is disclosed, and we recognise therein, in the province of art, one of the purest and freest productions of human creative power.

§ XXXVII.

MELODY.

TONES being given, and a suitable succession of tones having been fixed upon—by æsthetic judgment, in the further progress of cultivation; by theoretic rule, on the introduction of art—and rhythm having acquired a legal definiteness, the possibility of the representation of the feelings was objectively grounded. The combination of tones to a whole was next required, and thus the representation itself was brought about. As a thought develops itself in representations and words, and by these means the contents of the same are wrought out, so that we can speak of thought pictures, and forms of thought, so a feeling and its tones become a picture and a phenomenon, and we describe the combinations of tones with regard to their succession and association as tone pictures. Language, in accordance with its acknowledged right, has recourse to a terminology which, emanating from the ideas associated with vision, is transferred to the sense of hearing, therefore it must not be regarded as an offence if, in that which follows, we speak of contemplation in the province of the Audible. This can only mislead those who are but little practised in abstractions, and truly in this respect, no slighter errors of judgment have been induced than, for instance, when in speaking of thoughts, it has been assumed that music has to represent the real and immediate thoughts of the understanding.

§ XXXVIII.

In the elucidation of the nature of music, no point can be more important than the enquiry as to what it is that we call melody. All theoretical treatises proceed from the assertion that the combination of tones may be regarded in a twofold manner, that when sounding successively they form melody, and when simultaneously they form harmony; and thus a duple science of Melody and Harmony becomes practicable. Nevertheless, for Melody, or the Science of Melodic, but little has been done; and if, in respect of the value and laws of melody, sundry ideas have been advanced, still a free and deep investigation has not been possible, for the reason that men are not agreed or clear as to what it is that constitutes Melody. Writers lost themselves in discussions concerning the validity of melody and harmony, and the subordination of the one to the other, and vainly built without a foundation. Therefore, in order to avoid increasing the confusion of language, it is before all necessary to elucidate a fundamental idea; having at the same time regard for that which has hitherto been attempted on this subject. As an ancient truth we find recorded in treatises, and generally accepted, that Melody is a pleasing or agreeable succession of tones. But it will at once appear that the idea of that which is pleasing is far too general, and has merely been afterwards adapted to the nature of the subject, for not every pleasing succession of tones can be regarded as melody, and we also meet with melodies that are displeasing and not beautiful. We do not attain to more definite results when Sievers terms melody a definite motion or flowing succession of feeling tones, for we are naturally led to enquire into the signification of the word *feeling*, and are rather inclined to imagine that a definition of music in general is intended. Another error arises from the confusion of melody with expression. This occurs in the case of Sulzer who finally understands nothing more than characteristic delineation, which, surely, attaches itself to melody in a secondary degree, but does not primarily constitute the same. The best of melody may be produced, and yet not attain to characteristic life and beauty in representation; and to how many melodies must expression be denied. Not a few, with the intention of avoiding the admixture of foreign ideas, held fast to the word Succession, and placed melody in antithesis to harmony, reasoning that the latter represents the constancy, or the enduring condition of the spirit, while the former represents progressively the variations of the inner emotions. But progression is not excluded from harmony, nor is this confined within itself, for there are a vast number of harmonies which demand a progression, without which they could not be accounted as dissonances. And does not melody exist at the root of all harmony? On the other hand, the ascending and descending scale would, on this supposition, constitute a melody. Krause and others imagined to have discovered a way out of these difficulties, when they taught that melody speaks the feeling of a single heart, the voice of a single individual; whereas harmony contains a number of voices. This opinion, however, can only mislead still further, for, in the first place, there lies in each representation but one individuality, and the song of many parts can only be regarded as the union of several individualities; then again the polyphonic song and music in chords always follow the laws of harmony, consequently we again return to the unsolved point of commencement.

Just as little was gained by insufficient comparison, as, for instance, in the case of Wagner, who wrote (*Musikalische Zeitung*, 1823, p. 719), 'Melody is the material of music as colour is of painting.' Thus men lost themselves in the Indefinite, and even Gottfried Weber stated in the *Encyclopædia* ii. 2, p. 299 : " If the succession of tones be in accordance with the rules of art, that is, if it have a musical meaning, it is called melody and—as we thereby imagine a person—a voice."

With a closer proximity to a correct definition, but with an evident absence of mature consideration, melody was described as that which can be sung, and this feature was ascribed to melody as its most important characteristic. From this idea emanated the general and oft-repeated demand that composers should adapt their musical productions to vocal performance, and obtain, from instruments, effects similar to those of the human voice. But its import was not expressed by the idea of that which is singable, which is too ambiguous and vacillatory. What, may we ask, is in general to be understood by this suitability to vocal performance? Surely not that which it is easy for mankind to sing? How can we reconcile herewith the oft-repeated observation, that harmony effects nothing without melody? How could it be remarked, as has not seldom been the case, that melody is obscured by too great fulness of harmony? When in ancient times church songs existed without melody, were they not suited to vocal performance? These and other questions are unanswerable by the theory of Cantabile.

§ XXXIX.

In order to solve the problem now before us, we must regard another searching, and, in music, essentially effective faculty of the soul. The inner life which is comprised by the feelings, in other words, that which is felt, must, in order to attain to expression, become a picture and suited to contemplation. Without this adaptation to contemplation, no representation,—

which requires an elaboration into a definite form—can be attained to; and it is, if not Beauty itself, still the forerunner and basis of Beauty. The force of the imagination lends this comprehensible imagery for the inner and outer senses. Tones, then, or a succession of tones in which feeling asserts itself in a manner suited to contemplation—that is, in definite form, clearly and purely—we call Melody, which, in the case of the formative arts, is in general described as suitability to contemplation, and constitutes the primary æsthetic form. Melody is, therefore, the successive combination of tones in an æsthetic, that is, in a comprehensible form. This is, however, contained both in tonal and in rhythmical relations, for, in both, the power of the imagination arranges and forms a picture, which, by according with the feelings, can and must awaken the same feeling in the listener. The rhythmical relations must not, however, be regarded as of less importance, and if those who speak of the effectiveness of rhythm in the representation of the Beautiful are silent as to how rhythm acquires this power of representing the Spiritual, or feelings, or æsthetic ideas, it would be well that they should give particular attention to the point which now comes under consideration.

§ XL.

SIMILARLY as in the poet, and the poem of his production, the representation of a thought, if it shall not obliterate itself, must become a comprehensible picture, and give birth to thought pictures and word pictures; so the power of the imagination converts a feeling into pictures of feeling, and tone pictures, and lends shapes to the same, in purely developed forms and their unity. Thus even tones, as the expression of the feelings, acquire objectivity, and may be compared with the representations of the lyric poem. By reason of the intuitive nature of music, it occurs, greatly to its advantage, that the inner tones of the spirit do not require, for their elucidation and definition, to be previously converted into visible forms, nor, as in poetry, does an elaboration of the subjects of the feelings take place, but the inner life immediately presents itself in a form, and the motion of tones expresses, without any mediation, the emotion of the soul. Such suitableness to contemplation renders it possible that the truth of the feelings may be expressed, and that Beauty may be attained to. The unity which the definite and pure forms bring about in the Comprehensible retains firm hold of that which exists in the feelings, and thereby a definite expression of the inner condition of the Soul is attained to, through which the inner emotion in its veracity becomes so prominent that it can penetrate into every alien spirit and excite similar feelings therein. We follow the melody as it passes from tone to tone, and with facility grasp it in its purity. This appropriation is assisted by the naturalness and definiteness of the same, and thus we immediately recognise the language of the human heart. Still melody does not in general contain only the expression of the soul, but expresses also individuality; its simplicity adapts it to the representation of particularities, and only the definite form of the melody grasps the peculiarity of an individual human heart. Comprehensibleness is such an essential condition of, and foundation for, beauty that it is very often confounded with the Beautiful itself. We shall hereafter consider what position it occupies with respect to Regularity, and to what extent the Beautiful is based upon the Comprehensible: here we have merely to remark that music without melody cannot under any circumstances be beautiful, and that melody is by no means lacking in beautiful combinations of harmony. Men speak of that which is pleasing in melody; and require to find a pleasing form therein. This is nothing more than the Comprehensible, which, however, does not always offer that which is pleasant of sound or delightful to the ideas. For a melody may stand the test, and consequently be genuine and good, and yet not flatter the ear, and men may even content themselves with that which is easy of contemplation, and consider it to be beautiful. This finds confirmation in Russian folk-songs, if one hears them sung naturally and not from notes. Even the Ugly may be suited to contemplation and thereby become æsthetically useful. From these premises we are able to explain the common idea of the subject, for when melody is described as that which is adapted to vocal performance, or that which is vocally rich, only the pure and therefore easily comprehended form, in which feeling speaks immediately and truly to the heart, can be meant.

§ XLI.

FROM the nature of melody, we perceive the foundation of the demands which are made upon it, and its highest perfection, by Art. We here specify them, in order that it may become quite clear that in melody is contained that which is comprehensible in musical representation; still we adhere firmly to the statement that in melody, regarded for itself, neither Beauty nor Characteristic Expression must be pre-supposed, for these appear later. Consequently, it is not easy to give illustrations from existing art works, which aim at beautiful representation. That which musical treatises observe on this head, is, for the most part, confined to the treatment of several voices proceeding parallel to one another; while that which concerns the formation and development of melodic figures, is left to the taste which decides, without grounds, whether a melody sounds well or otherwise. With respect to that which melody on the whole should offer, theory has not concerned itself, nor has it taken into conderation such individual progressions as appear correct, or, at least, not unpleasant, and yet when combined as a whole do not please. Comprehensibleness exists by outer and inner unity, through the definite and clear development of sensuously comprehensible forms. Melody must therefore (1) contain a diversity combined to an unity. Two tones produce no melody, but three may, as Rousseau has shown in his well-known *air de trois notes*. Diversity of tones is suited to the reception of Beauty; unity arranges the whole for more certain comprehension. It will of course be understood that the compass may be very various. Short melodies confine themselves to the sphere of a single key (*ton*), or interchange only with near keys. That which here binds and unites is the relationship of nearer or remoter kind. It is (2) presupposed that an inner condition of agreement is in force, whereby, from a so-called fundamental tone, the successsion of related tones develops itself. This induces an inner cohesion, an organic formation. Both diversity and inner cohesion are united in Modulation, which admits of transition into other keys, but still always in accordance with the rules of relationship. Here one key serves for a basis, from which the progressions modulate, now upwards and now downwards, but return again to the original key. This key is at the same time the point of rest for the beginning and the end. Therein the definite outline of the tone figure is produced, in which the free motion of Beauty finds more or less room. If the Characteristic be added through the key or other means, the melody becomes expressive. Franklin tells us that the Scotch songs are for the most part excellent melodies, and have been retained so long in remembrance for the reason that they preserve a very strict modulation in connected consonances. On the other hand, melodies which, without any particular motive, contain foreign admixture, and are wanting in modulation, are to be rejected. We also find it difficult to play or sing them. But no elaborate proof is required of the falsity of the notion which regards modulation as being opposed to melody, seeing that this must move freely, for without modulation no melody can endure. (3) In the formation of tonal successions, rhythm obtains and lends keeping to the melody. From the fact that the succession of tones is definitely divided in time, and that to every part its place and external conditions are allotted, comprehensibleness is attained to. The compass of the melody must accordingly be rhythmically defined, and the time must mark out definite boundaries for the melody. We may compare herewith the outlines of a painting. Halting melodies are not seldom such as fail to please, because they are not properly arranged, and are therefore wanting in comprehensibleness; improve them rhythmically and they will pass for good melodies. Writers of Fugues sometimes imagine that all things must accommodate themselves to harmonic relations, and consequently give no attention to the parallel progressive melodies. The result is that their products are unwieldy and incomprehensible, and as such fail to gratify or displease. (4) Melody must offer Completeness, and must unfold that which lies within it. There are melodies which seem to be wanting in something; add but a few notes thereto and that which is censurable vanishes. The comprehensibleness labours under detriment when individual parts are wanting in the organic Whole, or do not stand out. If the melody shall serve for the representation of inwardly moved life, or for expression, it must be adapted to receive within it the thereto applicable expedients, and also to preserve thereby its completeness. (5.) From what we have already stated it will and must appear that a melody capable of standing a test is comprehensible. In ordinary language this is termed *singable*, and adapted to the human voice, or performable, and not borne down with technical difficulties. It is, however, obvious that that which cannot be sung or played does not and cannot exist in music. That which is merely relative need not here trouble us. The prohibitions of narrow theories, as, for instance, that against overstepping the octave, find no application in instrumental music, and the vocally practicable has been greatly extended and is always relative. We might, with greater show of reason, describe the property here spoken of as audible (*hearable*). That which is comprehensible and consequently easy of performance is the Intuitive and Pure. Where the ear, and consequently the voice also, cannot comprehend the unity, or where admixture renders comprehension difficult, where a clear construction of periods is wanting, there fails the so-called adaptability to vocal performance. The Whole of the melody must therefore have a thoroughly transparent organisation, and the parts must be so arranged that the mind is able to overlook the whole from points of rest, and to connect every single part of the whole. Everything indefinite or indistinct increases the difficulty of comprehension, and diminishes its intuitive character, or even entirely destroys it.

§ XLII.

MELODY has been termed the most essential element of music, and truly it is so, for without comprehensibleness, and without pure form of movement, no musical representation is sufficient, or is even possible. Therefore no opinion can be more thoughtlessly advanced, than, when in speaking of a composition, people say it contains melody also, as if this were merely an ornamental or accidental addition. Modern treatises, on the other hand, speak of the subordination of melody to harmony. From this arose the dispute which divided the Melodists from the Harmonists. The latter deny to melody a primary importance, and the former term purely melodious music paltry. Compare *Cæcilia*, Vol. vii., p. 269. According to this view of the matter, the representation of varying situations of the feelings, falls only to the part of successions of harmony, for people regard harmony as the mainspring of the whole, and even look upon melody as a disjointed harmony. On regarding the opinions which were advanced concerning the compositions of Paisiello,

Pleyel, Sterkel, and, at a more recent date, those of Rossini and Auber, it will be seen that the critics admitted their melodies to be clear, flowing, and excellent, but objected to the want of value in the whole, without considering that that which lessened its importance lay by no means in the melodies themselves, but in the nature and treatment of the same. The advocates of melody, of whom, by the way, not one has yet expressed himself as to what it is, remark, on the contrary, that the decisive effect of music rests almost always, and primarily, in melody, and that only in certain cases is it possible for harmony to attain to true and great effects, although its laws affect melody. See *Allgemeine Zeitung*, 28th year, p. 135. A greater uncertainty and confusion of language is nowhere more apparent than in this case. And yet it is possible to obtain a firm basis by means of a few fundamental definitions, which have in general been negligently overlooked.

§ XLIII.

MELODY was the earlier form of music, and, before developed art, music existed without harmony. To this day we possess melodies which deeply affect us, and to which no accompanying harmonies could be added without detracting from the pure effect. Certain songs do not require the assistance of harmony, while, on the other hand, no small number of modern songs depend wholly upon the predominating harmonies, and without them are meaningless, or at least too simple and transparent. It may readily be admitted that music which is wholly confined to melody, cannot satisfy us in ripened art, if the whole soul shall participate therein. With whatever truth it has been asserted that all melody follows the laws of harmony —however hidden they may sometimes appear,—with equal truth has it been said that harmony can only exist subject to the conditions and rules of melody.

Thus men have vacillated between unsolved problems; and the arguments which Nägeli advanced— far from impartially—against the theory of *cantabile*, can only be estimated from a point of view where a fundamental idea serves as a basis. Against the widely spread opinion that instrumental music is the imitator of the human voice, and that *cantabile* is the most essential requirement of all music, Nägeli advanced the paradoxical assertion, that the further instrumental music diverges in its turns, springs, augmentations, and diminutions, from *cantabile*, the more does it preserve its genuineness and perfectness. But neither experience nor theory confirms this view. In all music, whether it be that of instruments or of song, a pure comprehensible form must develop itself in the motion, and even instrumental music cannot dispense with definite, bounded, and naturally combined forms. It is not necessary that this form should be of such a character that the voice may follow it, but it should produce in the soul—however rich the grouping may be—a clear outline of a transparent picture for the contemplation of the senses. With all the artificialities of musical learning, a contrapuntally correct idea cannot attain to life if it lack the power of receiving in pure form the fulness of the soul.

From a less prejudiced point of view, melody and harmony were regarded as mingling with one another, inasmuch as the former gives comprehensiveness to the representation, which is also required by the progressions of harmony; on the other hand, the laws of harmony also contain the rules by which single succession of tones are constructed; still, this mutual penetration first made its appearance when music was constructed upon successions of chords, which merely hold the melody together and cause it to become comprehensible. Harmony is the Passive in music, and is set in motion by the melodic element; the single chord occupies the understanding in the combination of relations, but becomes, when subordinated to the comprehensibleness of melody, the expression of the feelings. In this respect the one-sided development of theory has obviously impaired the fundamental view. The laws of comprehensible representation, which are adhered to by music without harmony, should have been found; as, in the formative arts, the laws of delineation precede all others. But theory commenced with harmony without making the melodic element which it contains at all prominent, and consequently continued to build upon the laws of harmony alone, so that at last it was believed that melody was subject to the laws of harmony. From this fact we observe why theorists openly confess that in laying down rules for melody, they are able only to proceed negatively, and not positively, for at the most it is only possible to show which progressions are displeasing to the ear, and then indeed only with regard to the individual progressions of the parts, and not with respect to the delineation of the whole. Had they divided from the primary nature of melody that which constitutes the Beautiful, the Characteristic, and the Expressive in the same, they would also have been in a position to lay down rules for comprehensibleness and the rest. A melody may be empty and meaningless, and still offer a contemplatible Whole; while, whatever of a higher nature attaches to it belongs to the province of the Beautiful.

§ XLIV.

THE task of Melodic is to establish, arrange, and derive the pure forms of musical representation as they appear in simple and combined successions of tones, and consequently to point out in a science of form of musical representation the law of comprehensibleness, and to define the relationship and combination of the pictures. We do not as yet possess such a treatise, and great are the difficulties which place themselves in the way of its production, for the reason that the forms of the pictures appear before the imagination in a state of freedom which seems to defy all rule, but which, for all that, cannot exist without legality. Logic describes the fundamental forms and laws of thought, a science must do the same for the powers of the imagination and thus deliver up to us the foundation of melody. As regards tonal relations, the province is of great extent, inasmuch as melody passes into more distant relations than does harmony. The boundaries or fundamental relations, which it is necessary to define, may doubtless be reduced to numbers, as in harmony, and a vast number of problems still require solution which, if our ears may judge, will receive mathematical confirmation. Thus, for instance, the number four here also plays an important part. It is a rhythmical limit, and the dances of all nations are linked together in 4, 8, 12, 16 bars.

§ XLV.

HARMONY.

THE faculty which creates melody was referred to the power of the imagination, which forms the feeling to a comprehensible tone picture, and thus represents in tones. But the understanding also obtains and takes part in the general activity of the spiritual powers in the production of music, and creates Harmony. In order that we may not be misled, as many others have been, we shall not regard the word harmony as meaning euphony, or the unity of a musical work, but merely the arrangement and accordance of simultaneously sounding tones. Consequently harmony has a similar purpose to melody, viz., to establish the unity of a diversity of tones, but it attains to this result in another manner, not in the combination of a succession, but of simultaneous tones. Harmony is contained in a single chord, but that which combines diverse harmonies, blends them one with another, and is thus the means of producing a musical Whole, originates elsewhere,—it is melody which combines tones to a picture. Therefore we may regard a succession of harmonies as a combination of parallel melodies, or as a development of melody, whether it be that several voices in a chorus represent several individuals pervaded by the same feeling, but each in his character, or that various inner excitements are expressed in several voices. Even in the latter case, where different melodies may proceed with or against one another, melody holds them together, and forms their unity. Music, it is true, may, and did for a long time, consist of melody alone, when the man of nature found pleasure in expressing his feelings simply, in contemplatible tone pictures. But music became art, and combined, either by means of instruments or voices, that which was susceptible of combination, or a single time-form, and created, according to law and rule, the harmonic form which occupies amongst the inventions of the reflecting mind no inferior position. Rousseau alone was able, in his paradoxical partiality, to call it a barbarous Gothic invention, and to point out its origin in a want of appreciation for natural music. We, however, know historically that it constitutes a naturally progressive art development, and has grown with the human mind itself. The art of painting may serve for a comparison, which, for a lengthened period, was limited to mere successive representation and line perspective, until grouping admitted of a fuller arrangement, and the expressive delineation could operate with the perfected chiaro-oscuro. Through the above we have disposed of the question whether harmony is to be regarded as a concentrated melody, or melody as a diffused, and dismembered harmony. If the latter were true, everything which sounds well in succession would also sound well simultaneously, while only the reverse of this is the case, for not all melodic intervals adapt themselves to the pleasing unity of chords. Even though our existing music continues to build upon an harmonic basis, and to make use of harmonies melodically, so that the freely moving melodies may be referred to certain harmonic relations and forms, still we recognise therein a result of cultivated art, in which we judge of the relations which obtain amongst simple tones, according to fixed familiar forms.

§ XLVI.

IT has often been questioned whether harmony has its foundation in Nature, or is a product of the freely selecting human mind, appearing first in art. For instance, Knecht, acting upon Rameau's suggestion, endeavoured to show, in an essay which appeared in the *Musikalische Zeitung*, 1 Year, p. 129, that every tone bears within it its related tones, and that those sound simultaneously with it which stand in the nearest relation, so that with c, the fifth g and the higher third e are recognisable, or a piece of pine wood gives the large G, together with the small d, and b, similarly as upon the violin two tones produce a third, the so-called flageolet tone (Zeugeton). From these facts, and because there are natural bodies which produce chords, from which others are produced, men endeavour to prove that harmony has its foundation in Nature. But these facts are so uncertain, that Chladni, on finding that various bodies produce various modes of vibration, and consequently do not generate similar overtones, directly denied the general validity of a principle, and all knowledge tends to show that the production of musical harmony, by means of natural tones, is quite possible. If certain bodies, such as plates of glass and metal, contain, at the same time, diverse vibrations, and consequently produce several sounds simultaneously, it is then Nature that teaches us, and not human music, which was not derived from natural objects or creatures, for it is inadmissible to speak of a concert of birds in any other than a poetic sense. If a variegated admixture of high and deep tones produce a kind of wild harmony, then the wind whistles in harmonies through broken window-panes.

Nature possesses only melodic development. But in natural tone an unity of simultaneously sounding parts may occur, and this kind of harmony may be the natural, but we can only regard this as an element of tone. Whatever the natural tone may contain in a small way, and confined within itself, the human mind develops to a state of maturity, and thereby lends to music the clearly developed character of a co-operation of intellectual powers. Harmony appears in music under the enhanced participation of the understanding, which inspects, arranges, and balances, and is therefore only to be found in the more advanced periods of musical art cultivation. This assertion is not contradicted by the experiences which travellers relate to us concerning the savages, who make use of a second accompanying voice. This is a visible trace of awakening intellect. We indeed but seldom find in the songs of our lower classes that the accompaniment is placed in a deeper bass, or tenor voice, which, by advanced cultivation, is accounted as almost natural.

§ XLVII.

DID the ancient Greeks understand harmony? This question, so often investigated, has become a veritable bone of contention, and must still lack a definite answer, for the reason that we have diverged from the path of history. Conclusions as to the possibility of the matter prove nothing, and even the supposition that if less cultivated races accompany their songs in simple harmonic relations, probability is decidedly in favour of the highly cultivated Greeks having done so to, is wanting in a firm foundation, and is liable to deceive. Even the word itself has misled many, inasmuch as with the ancients the term harmony had a different signification to that which we are accustomed to attach to it. It is probable that for a long time the Greeks only made use of one-part music, in which many singers performed the same melody on the same tone or at the octave: the former—our unisono—they termed symphony, and the combination of different octaves antiphonies; but the ratios of the octave, fifth and fourth being fixed, and consequently a tone system, however faulty, being attained to, harmony resulted, for upon it this system is based. This the Greeks also termed symphony, which constituted a song of several parts, in addition to the combination in octaves. In strings tuned according to the tetrachord, the consonant intervals were present and were free to the performer. Moreover, it cannot be denied that the ancients possessed also a kind of figurate song, which could only be constructed upon an harmonic basis, although the latter was, perhaps, not theoretically established and developed. With this we may couple the assertion that the application of harmony was known to the Greeks, but that it was extremely simple and incomplete in character, and that harmony as a system was not established amongst them. We refrain from taking advantage of this opportunity to suggest, with certain philosophers, that the reason of this lay in the incompleteness of the not yet ripened feelings, for doubtless the ancients felt purely and deeply, and in ideal inspiration, but still in a different manner to Christian humanity. Here it will suffice to draw attention to the fact that in the remaining provinces, art forms have proceeded from simple and meagre beginnings to breadth and richness. But the cultivation of musical art proceeded but slowly, unlike the rapid development of the objective arts. This is confirmed by the imperfect instruments of ancient times, which—being struck or twitched—served merely for the rhythmical accompaniment of song. If, before the establishment of a definite succession of tones and of intervals, no complete harmony was possible, then the invention of instruments of the pianoforte kind, or of the organ—which were themselves the results of a craving for harmony—must have acted as a lever to the science of harmony. The organ of two octaves which was in use in the sixth century, perhaps afforded the first extensive survey, and whatever may have still appeared imperfect, became, on the introduction of temperament, a system of which the ancients, who made no use of thirds and sixths—regarding them as dissonances—could have formed no conception. With the tempered tone system, harmony also appeared in a practicable state. When, in the tenth century, or perhaps later (for every assumption as to an earlier origin is wanting in positive proof), the song of several parts was introduced by the English Bishop Dunstan, in place of the unisono, which was performed without fixed time measurement, unknown chords were produced, and, without the use of instruments, the vocal choir, which accompanied the song in several parts—for fourths and fifths were added—attained to a kind of harmony, which led to the establishment of chords, and their successions. They possessed these chords when, in the twelfth century, the thirds and sixths were adopted as a basis for the Pleasing, and the seconds and sevenths, and the augmented fourth were, at least, made use of as passing notes. The mensural or figurate song developed by Franco, of Cologne, could not have existed without harmony, and as also the method of combining the accompanying voices may have been acquired, the elements were present which first became important on the introduction of a theory. The age of harmonic music does not, consequently, extend beyond the thirteenth century, and the productions were highly incomplete. Even in the fourteenth century, musical works were constructed according to the rules of a theory of counterpoint, and were not likely to please upon performance; and as in every art obedience to authority had the effect of confining and limiting, the free development of theoretical music was delayed, until the Netherlanders, and amongst them Zarlino (1565), completed the foundation, by the establishment of the ratios of the major and minor thirds, and Palestrina confirmed the acquired theory by practical demonstration. And yet how timidly was the chord of the seventh introduced, of which the rules were first elucidated at the beginning of the eighteenth century.

§ XLVIII.

IN discussing these historical facts, it was our intention merely to prove the truth of the assertion that harmony is the product of the comparing and arranging intellect, which selects for the representation of the feelings definite fundamental forms which it establishes after mature consideration. With the feelings and the imagination, a regulated activity of the understanding is associated in the course of progressive musical development, so that the complete inner man becomes active both in hearing and creating music. This activity of the understanding does not treat of objects in ideas, but compares, combines, and arranges relations; the understanding counts and calculates in music as Leibnitz tells us. Many attribute this to the feelings, which, however, cannot count, but merely comprehend unities. Others limited the assertion by stating that this activity of the understanding occurs without consciousness, or in the obscurity of an uncertain condition of the spirit. Certainly the consciousness which here obtains may be termed weak or obscure, but only for the reason that the understanding is subordinate to the feelings, or is overridden by the same, which make demands upon the entire consciousness. We comprehend that which is regular or concordant without becoming, at the same moment, conscious of the grounds and the procedure. Therefore we shall properly refer the proposition of Leibnitz (*Epist. ad Divers.*, Tom. i., ep. 154) to the simultaneous activity of the understanding and feelings, and observe the same in the case of harmonic music, nor shall we fail to understand the words of Maria Weber " Pure four part writing is the Cogitative (Denkende) in musical art."

Reichardt asserted, in opposition to Emanuel Bach, that the real art of music consists in becoming conscious of the inner and secret calculation of the soul; but Bach would not enter into this idea, perhaps because he imagined his maxim, "music must move the heart," to be endangered, And yet no small number of facts find their explanation in the assertion. We shall merely draw attention to the following:— (1) The reason that the most ancient music, as mentioned in the fables of Orpheus, Amphion, and Arion, produced such an incredibly powerful effect—notwithstanding that we can merely suppose thereby a simple melodic music—lies in the fact that the participation of the understanding was then but very trifling, if not entirely wanting, and consequently no limiting influence was exerted upon the feelings and powers of imagination. With mighty force, music bore the spirit with it in its course. Pythagoras was the first to regard, as essential, the activity of the understanding. (2) Is it not remarkable that the harmonic development of music falls precisely within that period in which the activity of the feelings predominated, and the subjective world of Faith and of Love rose into the broad light of day, namely, in the era of Christianity? But even then the understanding was drawn in to serve the one purpose. The ideas of religion, of devotion, or of love, taken up by the feelings, or converted into the same, required expression, and the totality of the powers of the soul was called into action; not a single spirit, but the union of many, the representatives of humanity, praised God's power and love. From this the understanding could not be excluded. Through it music became independent and acquired harmony, while no limitation was imposed upon the rights of the feelings. (3) Wherever feeling predominates, and the imagination asserts its freedom, melody prevails, even in compositions which might be considered learned. Italian music is distinguishable from German music, from the fact that, in the latter, intelligent harmony prevails, and we are so educated and accustomed to it that Italian music, by reason of its predominating melody, appears empty, notwithstanding its alluring sweetness. When therefore Italians justify the meagreness of Italian scores with the remark that music is not for the eye but for the ear, they should rather say that it is not for the understanding. (4) Men of feeling have but little perception for harmony; we may particularly observe this in the case of women, who seldom hear a fully scored symphony with pleasure, and turn from the strict style of ecclesiastical music as from an arid desert. On the other hand, we not seldom hear an inaptness to comprehend elaborate harmony excused by persons representing themselves as not being connoiseurs. He who speaks without possessing a knowledge of himself would do better by saying that his understanding is unsuited thereto. (5) Where the understanding is occupied too much, or solely, with music, apathy results, and compositions originating under such conditions are called dry, powerless, like compositions of Homilius. Thus the more modern music was, for a lengthened period, merely the product of the mathematically combining intellect. Double counterpoint may, doubtless, sober or render apathetic a sparkling fantasy, or an enthusiastically inspired temperament; but, on the other hand, a fugue, which originates in thought, may bear within it a peculiar charm. The listener follows the simultaneously progressive, the diverging, and meeting voices, compares and combines to an unity that which seems to be wanting in connection, or contrasting, and finds enjoyment in the varied activities of the thoughtful soul. (6) Harmony is acquired by study, and by means of it, works are created in which no single spark of genial inspiration exists; while the true masters of art in their ascent cast off the trammels of rule. Schicht said, respecting a Quartet of Beethoven, at the same time shaking his head, "All is good, only no logic," and he was both right and wrong. We possess with respect to harmony a sufficient theory, while melodic has neither been independently elaborate nor has it progressed beyond a number of negative cautions against certain errors. The older treatises of Baron and Nichelmann, who attempted to subject melody to a theory, are based upon harmony. The latter endeavoured only to show that those passages more particularly please in which, not only the melody, but the harmony, also, expresses the intention of the composer, support it, and cause it to be felt. (7) From a simple melodic thread, art has developed a complicated tissue, which may easily become entangled. It is quite natural that men should wish to return from these artificial combinations to the simplicity of Nature; therefore, in the progressive development of artificiality, a contention between Naturalists and Rationalists is inevitable; and we may be allowed the hope of seeing, at a future period, the attainment of the highest purpose, the gratification and elevation of the feelings.

§ XLIX.

ALTHOUGH we may now acknowledge that Harmony, as such, constitutes a product of the understanding and excites in the listener the activity of the understanding, still it has been stated, in that which we have laid before the reader, that we had no intention of asserting that it alone serves the understanding, unconcerned as to the primarily requisite expression of the feelings. He who makes use of it with the understanding alone, as is the case in scientific works, will not find his feelings affected, and he who regards composition as an arithmetical task has to do with musical numbers only. But if a connected succession of harmonies be really music, then a melodic development of the activity of the feelings is at the root of it. No combination of harmonies can be musically valid if it do not contain melody and progression in comprehensible forms. This even in the Choral. Vogler denied, but without reason, that melody could be attained to in the middle voices. Melody and Harmony penetrate one another, and their blended natures may be divided by abstractions, but in life they ever appear as an united whole, as long as arbitrary selection does not occur to disturb them. Harmony, therefore, melodically combined, may express feelings, and may become beautiful representation, and receive the ideal within it. That which falls to the lot of the faculties of proportion, must not prevent melodic effectiveness. If harmony were a combination of heterogeneous parts, the possibility of the representation of an individual feeling would be wanting, but it constitutes a combination of that which is related, and is consequently well adapted to express the unity of the feelings. A large sum of means is required to make the complete condition of soul comprehensible. But a strict definition of the idea is here necessary to guard against incorrect explanations.

In the *Cæcilia*, Vol. xii., p. 245, the following remarks occur:—Music does not only represent the inner occurrences by means of melody, but represents also, by means of harmony, a condition in which several feelings, as secondary feelings, are developed, which stand in some degree of relationship to the predominating feeling. In this distinction between occurrence and condition, the supposition that together with one feeling, which, for example, a song expresses, the accompanying harmony makes known, in the same moment of time, a number of other feelings which exist simultaneously in the soul, would be pyschologically and musically incorrect, for the conditions which gradually attach themselves one to the other, never occur but in change and succession, and not every individual tone in harmony expresses a particular feeling. But in such cases people ordinarily confound the polyphonic and accompanying music, which is subject to the laws of harmony, with harmony itself. In this kind of music it is quite possible to express a diversity of feelings in combination, or one and the same condition of spirit in several parts, and each in its individual manner, but the melodic law obtains therein; while the connection, as a matter of relation, falls to the part of the understanding. The unity which combines within it a great number of diverse tones can operate with greater effect, and by its greater breadth, increase also the amount of enjoyment. Thus harmony comports itself: both when it follows a melody by way of accompaniment, and when it operates independently and contains melody. The former occurs when a principal voice is given, to which others serve for closer definition and enforcement. Through harmonic accompaniment and development melody gains (1) in definiteness. In every key there are successions of tones which are also to be found in other keys. Consequently they are ambiguous. But if that be introduced which removes this ambiguity, and which definitely refers a succession of tones to a key, we attain to decisiveness which is necessary for a pure, comprehensible representation. Truly the melody itself may effect this, inasmuch as, in its further progress, it decides that which is questionable, but the picture is readily lost in such cases, and can never quite escape indefiniteness. A musical phrase may belong to C major or G major, to A minor or E minor, which it is quite evident cannot be a matter of indifference, by reason of the difference of expression. Then harmony is added, and, inasmuch as it limits the boundaries, it secures definiteness, and consequently the possibility of a particular expression results. We may also add different harmonies to one and the same melody, and give it other meanings; a song thus altered often appears to be an entirely different one, although the melody remains the same. Thus by means of harmony we attain to correctness of delineation and stricter definition of the tone-picture. And this even occurs with regard to the feelings, for therein ambiguity not seldom obtains, and we may ascribe to one and the same melody two different feelings. Harmony, then, to a certain extent brings thought to bear upon it, and removes that which is doubtful. (2) But harmony also secures fulness, both by quantity in the sum of the parts which are associated together, and by quality in expression. The use of a large mass of means to the same end must necessarily have an important effect. Although the feeling which expresses itself in, or is excited by, the melody may remain the same, still its delineation is more strongly marked by the unity of a combined mass of related tones; its power is enhanced, the delineation of the tone-picture rests upon a basis and obtains colour, and light and shade. Every song accompanied by harmony teaches us this, which, by reason of being richer in tones, also appears more expressive. It would be going too far to assert that a one-part song, or the performance of a single instrument incapable of producing chords, is unable to produce a sufficient effect, but it is certain that such effect would not be equal to that of an art-work in which several means are brought into operation. Harmony, however, is much more effective in an independent state. The sum of the related, although different voices, which are combined to an unity, compel, on the one hand, the activity of the combining understanding, and on the other hand gratify the heart, as much by the general concordance, as by the progressive motion under many modifications. The impression may become powerful when many voices combine to one fundamental feeling; ideal significance is attained to if the harmonies appear to be derived, not from the near reality, but from a higher world. This is peculiar to four-part music, which only exists through harmony. If we compare a movement of one of Beethoven's symphonies—which does not represent a single feeling, but a large tone-painting—with a painting like Raphael's School of Athens, or the Parnassus, we shall see that forms and motions associate themselves together in groups, to represent a fundamental idea, each separate item operates for a total impression, and yet each part asserts its individual value. Remotely or nearly related tones, which often appear to strive with one another, combine nevertheless to an unity, whose entire effect falls to the feelings, but whose relations are only comprehended by the intellect. If we adhere firmly to the fundamental idea, and do not permit ourselves to be led astray by the ordinary usages of language, the question, so often proposed since Rameau's time, whether melody or harmony be the most excellent or important, will find an immediate answer. A succession of harmonies becomes beautiful music only as a melodic succession, and notwithstanding the completions which have accrued to music through harmonic development, in the extension of its province, in the increase of the activity of the intellect, in a heightened independence, the primary basis ever remains the comprehensible and clear delineation of tone pictures. The prerogative of modern music is one that has been striven for, and rests upon the old unmoved basis. We combine several melodies, weave them together, resolve them, again combine them, and thus obtain extensive and diversely grouped tone-pictures in melodic movement for the expression of the moved inner life. Harmony and melody, which in this manner unite, stand not seldom in a relation of disparity. For instance, a work or phrase of melody may be esteemed excellent from its pure comprehensibleness, and may contain the Beautiful, while the succession of harmonies may be incorrect, or ordinary, or meaningless. We call to mind, many instances in the newer French operas. In works of more ancient date, the harmonies are interesting, while the melodies which form the basis of the same possess neither sufficient clearness of outline, nor depth of meaning. The reason of this is apparent in the fact, that, as regards the first case, the powers of the composer are not sufficient to produce further development, or fuller grouping, while in the second case, clearness of representation is wanting, and the understanding predominates or operates alone. This kind of music is termed learned, and may be understood or composed after a long course of study, but it may still be unadapted to the reception of Beauty, and may be based upon mathematically determinable relations. Fasch composed a sixteen-part Mass, in which each of the four-part choirs goes its own way, and yet form not only in themselves but conjointly, a grand unity elaborated in the minutest details. Such master works demand from the listener great facility of musical comprehension, consequently, universal comprehension can hardly be presupposed in such cases.

§ L.

SINCE Rameau's time, it has been repeatedly attempted to define the province of Harmony, and not only to include all possible combinations, but to arrange them systematically, according to the laws of their relationship. Truly, the combinations of tones must be regarded as numberless, but still their relationship may be determined and their proportions fixed. These endeavours gave rise to a science of chords (Accordenlehre)—if a combination of certain notes may be termed a chord—which we have also to regard from an æsthetical point of view. The province itself must also be known to us. Rameau, proceeding from the acceptation of simultaneously sounding tones, arranged the sum of the chords to a system, upon a basis of third and fifth. Marpurg, following up his efforts, divided the consonant and dissonant fundamental chords into two varieties, of first and second rank. In the first rank he placed the consonant and dissonant triads, in the second, the fundamental chords of the ninth, eleventh, and thirteenth, whereby a number of inversions were discarded as quite useless. Vogler, Kepler's tutor, attaching himself to Marpurg's theory, made use of the divisions of the monochord as a basis, and thus obtained the relations 1, 3, 5, and, by inversion, eight consonances. Chladni, on the other hand, arranged them according to the system established by Leibnitz and Descartes with regard to the number of vibrations, and obtained, as consonances, three fundamental chords, the triads in major and minor, and the chord of the dominant seventh, with minor seventh (c, e, g, b♭); as dissonances, the chord of the major seventh, which combines the major triad with the dissonance of the major seventh, that is, with the minor triad of its third. Gottfried Weber based all chords upon triads and chords of the seventh, which, being susceptible of inversion, developed new forms; and he thus accepts seven varieties, to which all the tone combinations which occur in music may be referred. Häfer, finally, attained to a simpler arrangement, inasmuch as he referred all chords to the combination of thirds, and accepted four species, the triads, and chords of the seventh, ninth, and eleventh. The various fundamental harmonies or chords are referred to the major and minor keys, or are defined by the size of the third, while those chords are peculiar to a key which may be constructed from the tones of its scale, whereby ambiguity obtains, inasmuch as the same chord may belong to various keys. In progression, the diversity increases to an extraordinary degree, so that Weber calculates the collective number of harmonies at 6,888, while Maas pointed out no less than 9,312 successions. How the division and establishment is proceeded with, and in what manner the various grades of relationship are determined—a succession with two notes in common, is nearer related than is a succession with only one—need not here concern us, we shall merely regard the æsthetic contents, and show how, in a combination based upon comprehensible relations, there exists the possibility of expressing feelings, and of securing inner gratification by means of beautiful representation. We shall, consequently, have less to do with the formation of single chords than with successions of chords, for a chord is doubtless musical, yet when regarded for itself is still no music, unless it be used between pauses, and consequently with relation to a succession. That which is musical in a single chord forms the unity, which is called consonance, and which may in itself please.

§ LI.

BUT what, may we ask, is a Consonance? This has ever been a difficult problem for theorists. Harmonies were divided into consonant and dissonant: to the former, were classed the major, minor, and diminished triads; to the latter, the chords of the seventh, and every other chord which contained a note foreign to the harmony; but the chord of the dominant seventh, with minor seventh, was regarded as a consonance. These dissonances were explained as that which, in music, sounds unpleasant, or at least not wholly pleasant, the consonances as that which sounds agreeable; but it was by no means clearly explained why music does not exist without such unpleasant sounds or dissonances, or why fine art does not endeavour to effect their removal. It was further found necessary to accept a species occupying a position between the two, and Fries called the dominant seventh (c, e, g, b♭) the characteristic seventh; it was also found necessary to recognise in the dominant chord, the combination of the consonance with the dissonant second and seventh, g b, d f. Weber adopted a contrary opinion, and denied the dissonance altogether, while amusing himself at the expense of the old theory, but he thereby engendered further disputes. Dissonance doubtless exists in accordance with conditions which have their foundation in the human organization, but not in music, that is, not in the progressive movement of tones, but only in the individual tone and the individual chord which is not pleasantly combined. Consonance and dissonance are effective harmonically, and are therefore both useful, and consequently pleasing after their manner. But all harmony either is, or strives to attain to, perfect unity, and in a chord several tones combine to the unity of one tone, which may be distinguishable in its several parts, yet forms but one collective tone. Consonance is the positive attainment of accordance and unity complete in itself, from which further unities may be derived. Dissonance is a prospective accordance, a still incomplete unity, in which it is not easy for the understanding to arrange the disparity of the relations. Therefore it cannot gratify of itself, but strives after completion and equalization. A transition into consonance is required, a so-called resolution is necessary, and in such development that which is unsatisfactory ceases to be so. Consequently, a dissonance or that which sounds unpleasant, can only occur in detached parts, or single chords, not in progressive music, wherein that which is antagonistic and unsatisfactory is always equalized, and the principle of unison is exhibited in a comprehensible manner, in difference and its removal. That which theorists advance as dissonance in progressive music, is either valid as consonance, or is intentionally made use of in a composition as characteristic expression. We have seen how the chords of music are also the chords of the soul, and their characteristics are gratifying and definite motion,—however excessive—and ungratified striving, and unequal motion. Our moved inner life, and consequently the feelings, consists of an uninterrupted alternation of antitheses of freedom and constraint, of elevation and depression, of gratification or non-gratification. Therefore harmonic music can only consist of combinations of chords suited to such expression, and must, for this reason, unite within it both consonant and dissonant elements, without ceasing to be pleasant of sound, and without being, in itself, disharmonic. Herewith, the old dispute as to what may be allowed and is useful is disposed of. Men may still assert that certain forms please the ear more than others, just as elliptical or circular forms are more pleasing to the eye, and may refer us to a peculiar organization of the ear, so that we are finally led to the conclusion that we are unable to decide *à priori* as to the usefulness of intervals and chords, but only after gaining experience of them; but the understanding invariably judges as to the propriety of the relations, although we may be unconscious as to the mode of procedure, and determines their forms according to an unknown law of Nature, and according to the state of intellectual cultivation, and has ever determined the same during the whole progress of intellectual development. Had the ancient Greeks possessed thirds and sixths, which they discarded as dissonances, in such purity as we now possess them, they would assuredly not have rejected them; but by reason of the then existing impurity, they were not unjustifiably set aside, and the Grecian ear had become so accustomed to the ratios then established that they did not desire an alteration. But when finally the ratios of the major and minor thirds were fixed by Zarlino, a greater degree of definiteness in general was attained to, notwithstanding the fact that the school of Palestrina avoided the thirds in cadences. The ear and the understanding follow the ratios of the tones and arrange them. Where the power of the ear for comprehension and distinction ceases, by reason of its national or individual difference of organization, the determination of tone ratios also ceases, and we are not in a position to determine the infinitely small variations. A long deliberation has measured out the whole province, and a fixed tone system has been established and its relations reduced to rule, within which not only the sense of hearing is sufficient, but the understanding, also, refers that which it is possible to determine to numbers, according to the vibrations which form the basis of all tones. Wherever the understanding is able to comprehend the simple ratios, the soul is gratified, and where, on the other hand, the feelings are in a state of gratification, or reflection, whether it be through joy or grief, they select for their expression, music in comprehensible relations, and this becomes harmonic consonance. But a long succession of equal consonances would be an untrue picture, and therefore unnatural, for the reason that all spiritual existence consists of the alternation of Becoming and Become (Werden und Seyn), of striving after and attaining to a certain condition. But the activity of the understanding always obtains; and erroneously should we dispute as to whether the foundation of dissonance should be considered an intellectual, or an æsthetic, when it is certain that the comprehension of the ratios (either with regard to the vibrations of air, or of the nerves, or of numbers) can only be accredited to the understanding. But, before all we must not forget that the understanding seizes upon much that it cannot develop to a perfect idea, or become clearly conscious of. It counts, calculates, and compares in the formation and comprehension of harmonic relations, without expressing itself. But we must seek for the reason of the use of dissonances not only in contrast and variety, but in the naturalness of the soul's activity, which attains to representation. When this exists in a state of simplicity, as in men of Nature, who are not uncultivated, we shall find that dissonances are used more seldom ; and the human ear must rather become accustomed to the same that it may not find therein that which is antagonistic to Nature.

§ LII.

THE sphere of the consonances which are now valid with us, lies within the ratios 1 to 6 and their duplication, and division into halves, and the limit is the number seven. Whatever extends beyond these numbers, as, for instance, 11, 13, 17, etc., we call dissonance. When Kepler attempted to discover the reason of this line of limitation, and showed that the exclusion of the large prime numbers arose from the fact that the delineation, in a circle, of equilateral and equiangular figures, of the numbers 11, 13, 17, is geometrically impossible, he could not have imagined that Grauss, after the lapse of years, would prove that the circle may be divided into 17 equal parts. All that remains for us to do, is to content ourselves with the law of Nature, which, through the organization of the ear, imposes upon the comparing and arranging intellect a limit to its comprehension of unity. But in the chord, not only the single tone comes under consideration, but the relation of all combined tones, and thus a large sum of differences of degree arises, the analysis of which is left to theory, for two tones, which in themselves are consonant, may enter into a relation of disparity, when one or two others are added, that is, are combined to one chord. It will readily be perceived how falsely many formerly took for granted, that the higher or highest note contained the particular which causes the dissonance, for another note frequently is the cause of it. We may here omit a specification of the consonances which theorists divide into perfect and imperfect, or fundamental and derived, and the dissonances which are distinguished as essential or accidental The relation is in all cases merely relative, inasmuch as the approximation, through definite relations of vibration, to the most perfect consonance consists only of a difference of More or Less. A mitigation of dissonance is secured through preparation, and this is the more becoming, the more difficult the combination of the dissonance may be; it is necessary in the case of suspensions. Similarly, the necessity for progression is obvious, and the craving for a resolution increases, in various degrees; in the case of different chords, so that we are able to classify them according to these degrees; the freedom of passing into other near or remote chords is various, being greatest in the case of consonances, and small in that of dissonances. But the progression of harmonics is most naturally limited to the circle of near relations, and that which is remote can only be introduced by means of mediatory chords. To what extent the degree of dissonance may be enhanced without becoming inadmissible, is taught by the fundamental law of characteristic beautiful representation, of which we shall have occasion to speak hereafter. An extension of this sphere could only take place in the later periods of art development. On the other hand historians err, when they make the use of dissonances dependent upon the invention of means to resolve them, for with dissonance the means of its resolution is given by Nature. The combination of notes to a chord, we know by experience to be limited to a certain number. There are no chords of six parts, and when six different tones sound simultaneously one or more is always so dissonant, that the ear can only tolerate it as a transitory suspension. Five-part chords can be used independently. Still the ear is able to grasp correctly 16 or 20 parts at the same time, so that a strict distinction is possible, as may be proved in the case of good music directors, who are able to detect an error of a single part. But the reason thereof does not lie in the ability of the ear to comprehend a great deal, but in the perception of the relations of unity.

§ LIII.

FREE PLAY IN TONE-PICTURES.

FROM the observations which we have hitherto made, it appears that in music, and through the same, while the inner activity of the feelings becomes a tone-picture, in successions of tones, and in groups of harmonies, the powers of the imagination are rendered active in the production of comprehensible forms, and the understanding, likewise in the comprehension of the proportions of the same. Herewith, however, the nature of music is not finally exhausted. When we regard a feeling as a condition, it might be thought that a single tone or a single chord is sufficient for its delineation; but feeling knows no state of rest, and is continually kept in a state of excitement; it is not even exhaustible; it therefore chooses for its representation a number of suitable tones, or delineates the moved living picture by means of a number of combined tones in free motion, similarly as the painter represents passive forms by means of lines and colours. When man, in representing his inner self, rises to art, and endeavours to create a musical work, the first thing which operates to this end is the free play of the fantasy, which evolves tone-pictures for the expression of the feelings. Music becomes a play of tones, and therein the character of the spirituality is wrought out, inasmuch as in the representation of the feelings, the creative fantasy takes part, and resolves the one feeling which fills the spirit into numerous picture forms. It then elaborates the material of the inner condition of soul, which is presented to it in a play of tones, and by reason of its free spiritual activity, delights and satisfies if it causes a similar play of the powers of soul in the listener.

§ LIV.

THE troublesome question as to the import of music is thus disposed of. We truly cannot tell what every individual tone in a piece of music says, as is possible in the case of the words of language, or even what feeling is expressed in particular harmonics; but in the condition of the feeling—which in itself is not indefinite—the fantasy operates, and creates and combines melodic and harmonic tone-pictures, which not only represent that condition, but are also, in themselves, valid as representations. Thus, for instance, the feeling of perfect enjoyment of life, or of sadness, becomes a picture in a Rondo, or in an Adagio, in which all individual successions of tones, and forms of tones, are in unison with the fundamental feeling. Such free play was considered by Nägeli to be the most important element of music, but thereby he was led to adopt a one-sided opinion, and to deny the definite expression and character of music. Play (Spiel) is indeed its nature, but not its only nature, or, as Nägeli says, its ultimatum. After such an opinion we need not wonder at the assertion which he subjoins (see page 33 of the Lectures), that a Prelude, a Waltz, and a Symphony, all say and effect the same thing, and that Art plays everything out of the soul instead of into it. We must admit that music in its pure forms is but a play of tones, which certainly does not express the ideas, or that which is definite in thought, but nevertheless allows a moved inner life to become comprehensible. Let us take, for example, a composition of Meyerbeer, say his Sixth Quartet, Op. 33, or his Variations for Violoncello and Pianoforte, in which latter the fundamental feeling of a perfect delight in life expresses itself, and even continues to be heard through a softer strain of sadness, and attests the peace of the soul, but all in a free play of the fantasy, in which but little demand is made upon the understanding. This effect lies in the whole—which consists of manifold tone-pictures—and not in the individual parts of the psychological contents, which become contemplatible; and we do not crave after comprehensible import, for the play of tones transplants us into the same state of feeling, and thus verifies the contents. But music may degenerate and become mere empty play, serving only for sensuous excitement. It then lacks meaning. This is the kind of music which Nägeli described in a general way as having no contents. He had in his mind's eye instrumental musical works in which we find nothing further than a superficial play of tones, which are constructed and held together in accordance with certain rules of composition, without a trace of a requisite foundation in the feelings. Our time produces numerous examples of the same,—works without power and life, partly in mere hashed-up forms of which Mozart was in the habit of saying "there's nothing in them." What were the greater part of the compositions of Gelinek and Hofmeister than this? What the recently published quartets of Rossini?—to say nothing of the heartless and soulless compositions of our own manufacture (Variations, Potpourris, &c.), with which so-called *virtuosi* travel from town to town. They can only be called players (Spielleute) and their performances play (Spiel). France has provided us with this kind of music in great abundance. The connoisseur turns from such emptiness with disgust, and even he who merely desires entertainment cannot tolerate such music at all times. Compositions of this kind only remain in favour for a time by reason of their fashionable titles, or the dexterity which is required in their performance. We may compare herewith the poetry, which not seldom offers a mere empty play of the fantasy, such as was in vogue amongst us Germans during the period of the trifling of Jacobi and Glenn, and of the meaningless Romance of the school of Schlegel. If a play of tones shall gratify, it must be intellectual. What this may mean art-philosophy must explain. We require, namely, in a musical art-work a play of tones, which even in the freest motion bears within it a meaning, and an animation of an intellectual kind. With such high demands, that which merely excites the sense of hearing and, being soulless, does not address the soul, is condemnable. But with less strict requirements, we may admit the validity of music, which, in the development of melodic forms, gives itself up to the sportive fantasy. Thus, for instance, folks melodies even although they offer no marked characteristic expression, are to be esteemed, and may be likened to the folks songs such as are collected in the "Boy's Magic Horn" ("Des Knaben Wunderhorn").

On the other hand, Mozart and Haydn, Bach and Hasse, each plays after his own intellectual manner. Sebastian Bach, if we may place one of them before the others, is rich in sport of the fantasy, particularly in his pianoforte works, but he does not content himself with sensuous gratification, nor aim at mere flattering allurement, but invariably allows the activity of the understanding to play its part, and, without necessarily becoming dry or cold, conveys gratification to the spirit.

§ LV.

MODIFICATION OF EXPRESSION.

FREE activity of the spirit not only makes itself known in the play of tone-pictures, but also manifests itself in the varied increase and diminution of force, whereby a modification of expression becomes possible. The human tone, whether it be from the throat of a man, or from an instrument, possesses— although in a less degree in the case of twitched instruments and instruments of percussion—an elasticity which becomes apparent to us in the growth, or in the strengthening of a tone, or in the decrease or weakening of its fulness and power. This is the dynamic property of tones. Through the same, that is, through a rising and falling, not only the involuntary ebb and flow of the inner life is made known, but an arbitrary arrangement of the expression becomes possible to the free intellect. Thus a double operation is in force; firstly, the musical accentuation and articulation of tones, and, secondly, the increase and diminution of tone. We will embrace the opportunity here offered for a general explanation, in order to secure a firm basis for our entire theory: namely, in no case does greater ambiguity and confusion prevail than with regard to the idea and definition of accent. Sometimes the quantity of the rhythmical length has been erroneously drawn into the idea, while no regard has been given to the difference which exists between $- \smile$ and $\stackrel{\prime}{-} -$; or that which falls to the part of comprehensibleness has been confounded with that which constitutes the expression and colour; and for the most part the accent, which in song accords with the word accent, has been kept in view.

§ LVI.

THE More or Less, the Stronger or Weaker, or the intensive character of tones, serves in musical representation a threefold purpose, which we shall here distinguish as twofold, inasmuch as the increase of strength may occur in the case of a single tone, or of a succession of tones. In both cases, the increase of strength, which in a broader sense we term accent, offers a means of clearly delineating the true expression of the inner life, and for the production of Beauty. The comprehensibleness is enhanced, for through this difference of weakness and strength, individual parts of the tone-picture may be rendered prominent, or be thrown into the shade, and thus a clearer arrangement be attained to. This unites itself with the Rhythmical, in which already the alternation of length and brevity of time duration operates effectively. In this alternation the increase of strength occurs in the case of certain successions of tones, both at the beginning of definite rhythmical members and forms, and in free melodic accentuation. Thus it occurs that individual parts, members, and figures of the tone-painting are distinguished, whereby the rhythmical proportions are more easily measured, and the arrangement of the whole comprehended with greater facility. If the accent as cæsura opposes various members one to the other, if it causes contrast, and gives to various parts light and shade, then the greatest effect of music is attained to. Thus the accent of rhythmical members gives to dance music an animation which continues without a check, notwithstanding the symmetrical nature of the time. A second result attained to by the increase of tone, is the true expression of the feelings, in which certain particulars affect us more strongly than others, and take firmer hold, while others are limited in strength, or excite but slightly. We shall regard this subject more closely in our investigations concerning expression. Finally, accentuation is serviceable in the representation of formal and characteristic Beauty, inasmuch as through its various grades, a free motion is sustained, while that which is peculiar becomes prominent in proportion to the extent of its intensive value. Of this also we shall treat more copiously elsewhere.

§ LVII.

THE increase and diminution of tone, the portamento of the voice, the slurring and sustaining of tones, and whatever else men are accustomed to term the forms of a performance, in which the connection and blending of tones conveys a true impression of the inner emotion, are peculiar to the music of mankind, for the reason that they result from free intellectuality and ideality. Similarly, as we regard the play in tone-pictures as a free play, which is animated by the spirit, so the modification of tone appears as a free domination over tones. Man alone animates tones, and breathes into them a higher life, and we say of his music that it is full of soul; we should rather define it by the word ideal, for, in the combination and blending of tones, ideality is evinced, both in the represented continuity, and in the softening down of the sharp lines of demarcation. The growth and cessation of tones does not operate as the sum or compass of the increased or diminished tone, for in this case the strongest and weakest would be the most perfect, but it operates symbolically. Through the same, is represented the striving after infinity, and the cohesion of all details through infinitely small parts, and a faint notion is excited of that which is not attained to by the strongest, and does not disappear in the weakest tone. Thus it is a reflection of the idea which delights us, and our reasoning powers are excited to ideas by the animation of tones, while the feeling which thus becomes audible, and echoes in the listener, is an ideal feeling.

§ LVIII.

THIS leads us immediately into a larger and higher province, and to the third particular, in which the spirituality of music evinces itself, viz., TO ITS SUB-ORDINATION TO THE IDEA OF BEAUTY. In this is united all that has been hitherto advanced, for that which we have termed the expression of the feelings, the activity of the powers of imagination, the participation of the understanding, and the co-operation of reason, appears now in the full light of Beauty, as that which is pleasing to the mind, and ideal. It may be that either the comprehensibleness of melody, or the proportionableness of harmony, or the free play of the fantasy prevails, and determines the character of the musical work, and gratifies us more or less; but for all that the general requirements for an art-work remain the same, viz., that it shall be a beautiful work, and that that which is spiritual within it must immediately address the spirit. Herewith the art-work is produced and completed. How this occurs we will endeavour to show in the following book.

END OF BOOK THE FIRST.

CATALOGUE OF PUBLICATIONS

Issued by **WILLIAM REEVES,**

LITERARY, ART AND MUSIC.

ALSO

WORKS ON FREEMASONRY.

Published and Sold by
W. REEVES, 83, CHARING CROSS RD., LONDON, W.C.

Just Ready.   8vo, boards, Price 1/6.

"THUS SPAKE ZARATHUSTRA"

By F. NIETZSCHE, *A BOOK FOR ALL AND NONE*, TRANSLATED BY THOMAS COMMON, containing Zarathustra's Prefatory Discourse, with Critical and Bibliographical Notices, Part I.

"*Nietzsche's Ethics, however, are not the Ethics for boys, nor for old women, nor for dreamers either; they are the Ethics for full grown men, for noble, strong, wide-awake men, who shape the world's destiny.*"
—EDITOR.

Just Published.   Cr. 8vo, Limp Cloth, 2s.

THE ART OF MODULATING.

A SERIES OF PAPERS ON MODULATING AT THE PIANOFORTE. WITH 62 MUSICAL EXAMPLES. By HENRY C. BANISTER.

Not only at Examiations—*viva voce*—but in Actual Experience, is ability required to pass rapidly, with very little "process" form one key to another, &c.

Just Published.   Thick Crown 8vo. Cloth, Price 7/6.

THE LIFE OF HENRY GEORGE.

Author of "Progress and Poverty,"
With Portraits.   By his Son, HENRY GEORGE, JUN.

Just Published.   Thick Crown 8vo., Cloth 10s.

Important Critical Contribution.

CHOPIN: THE MAN AND HIS MUSIC.

BY JAMES HUNEKER,

Author of "MEZZOTINTS" in Modern Music.

. . . . Mr Huneker is a Chopin enthusiast. He accords admiration to Brahms, to Wagner, to Tschaïkovsky: his worship is reserved for Chopin. Being gifted with clear insight and imagination which grasp many and diverse moods Mr. Huneker is a sane critic and a manly. . . . . There is no pretence at new material in the book. Mr. Huneker has garnered all that has been written about the composer and he has threshed out the grain from the chaff. The result is, therefore, of value. . . . . The story of Chopin's life, it may be said, is clearly and interestingly told by the author. In a short space it is the best life of Chopin I know, just as the latter half of the book, on the music, is the most comprehensively critical account of the composer's achievements.—*Musical Standard.*

LARGE EDITION, over 1,000 pp., imp. 8vo.

CHAFFERS (Wm.), MARKS AND MONOGRAMS ON EUROPEAN AND ORIENTAL POTTERY AND PORCELAIN, with Historical Notices of each Manufactory, preceded by an Introductory Essay on Ancient Pottery and on the Vasa Fictilia of England and Mediæval Earthenware Vessels, with over 3,500 Potters Marks and Illustrations, revised and edited by F. Litchfield, ornamental cloth, Ninth Edition, with Additional Information and Marks, 42s.

EIGHTH EDITION, CONSIDERABLY AUGMENTED AND CAREFULLY REVISED BY A. MARKHAM.

CHAFFERS (W.), HALL MARKS ON GOLD AND SILVER PLATE, Illustrated with Revised Tables of Annual Date Letters employed in the Assay Offices of the United Kingdom, 346 pp., roy. 8vo, cloth, 16s.

This edition contains a History of the Goldsmith's Trade in France, with extracts from the decrees relating thereto, and engravings of the standard and other Marks used in that country as well as in other foreign States. The Provincial Tables of England and Scotland contain many hitherto unpublished Marks; all the recent enactments are quoted. The London Tables (which have never been surpassed for correctness) may now be considered complete. Many valuable Hints to Collectors are given, and cases of fraud alluded to, etc.

CHAFFERS W.), COLLECTOR'S HANDBOOK OF MARKS AND MONOGRAMS ON POTTERY AND PORCELAIN OF THE RENAISSANCE AND MODERN PERIOD, selected from his larger work, New Edition Revised and considerably Augmented by F. Litchfield, Twelfth Thousand, 234 pp., post 8vo, cloth, gilt, 6s.

THE COMPANION TO " HALL MARKS ON GOLD AND SILVER PLATE."

CHAFFERS (W.), GILDA AURIFABRORUM, A History of English Goldsmiths and Plateworkers and their Marks stamped on Plate, copied in *facsimile* from celebrated Examples and the earliest Records preserved at Goldsmiths' Hall, London, with their names, addresses and dates of entry, 2,500 *Illustrations;* also Historical Account of the Goldsmiths' Company and their Hall Marks and Regalia; the Mint; Closing of the Exchequer; Goldsmith Bankers; Shop Signs, a

Copious Index, etc., a New Edition, 267 pp., roy. 8vo, cloth, 12s.

CHAFFERS (Wm.) HANDBOOK TO HALL MARKS ON GOLD AND SILVER PLATE, with Revised Tables of Annual Date Letters Employed in the Assay Offices of England, Scotland and Ireland, Edited and Extended by C. A. Markham., *F.S.A.*, cr. 8vo, cloth, 5s.

MARKHAM (C.), HANDBOOK TO FRENCH HALL MARKS ON GOLD AND SILVER PLATE. Illustrated. Crown 8vo, cloth, 5s.   1900

The above 2 works, in conjunction with CHAFFERS' HANDBOOK complete the set of HANDBOOKS.

MARKHAM (Chr. A., *F.S.A.*), HANDBOOK TO FOREIGN HALL MARKS ON GOLD AND SILVER PLATE (except those on French Plate), containing 163 stamps, cr. 8vo, cloth, 5s.

COBBETT (W.), RURAL RIDES in the Counties of Surrey, Kent, Sussex, Hants., Wilts., Gloucestershire, etc., edited with Life, New Notes, and the addition of a copious Index, New Edition by PITT COBBETT, *map and portrait*, 2 vols, cr. 8vo, xlviii. and 806 pp.), cloth gilt, 12s. 6d.

Cobbett's "Rural Rides" is to us a delightful book, but it is one which few people know. We are not sure that up to the present time it was impossible to get a nice edition of it. We are therefore glad to see that Messrs. Reeves & Turner's recently published edition is a very creditable production, two handy well-filled volumes:—*Gardening*:

KEATS (John), THE POETICAL WORKS OF JOHN KEATS (large type), given from his own Editions and other Authentic Sources, and collated with many Manuscripts, edited by H. Buxton Forman, *portrait*, SIXTH EDITION,   8 pp., cr. 8vo, buckram, 8s.

LONG (W. H.), A DICTIONARY OF THE ISLE OF WIGHT DIALECT, and of Provincialisms used in the Island, with Illustrative Anecdotes and Tales, etc., Songs sung by the Peasantry, forming a Treasury of Island Manners and Customs Fifty Years Ago, 182 pp., post 8vo, cloth, 2s. 6d.

MALTHUS (T. R), AN ESSAY ON THE PRINCIPLE OF POPULATION, or a View of its Past and Present Effects on Human Happiness, with an Inquiry into our Prospect respecting the Future Removal or Mitigation of the Evils which it Occasions, Ninth Edition, 567 pp., 8vo, cloth, 8s.

SHELLEY LIBRARY (The), An Essay in Bibliography, by H. Buxton Forman, Shelley's Books, Pamphlets and Broadsides, Posthumous Separate Issues, and Posthumous Books, wholly or mainly by him, 127 pp., 8vo, part I, wrappers, 3s. 6d.

SHELLEY (Percy Bysshe), THE POETICAL WORKS OF (in large type), given from his own Editions and other Authentic Sources, collated with many MSS., and with all Editions of Authority, together with his Prefaces and Notes, his Poetical Translations and Fragments, and an Appendix of Juvenalia, Edited by H. Buxton Forman, Third Edition, with the Notes of Mary Wollstonecraft Shelley, *fine etched portrait*, 2 vols., cr. 8vo, cloth (with Design in Gold on cover by Rossetti), 12s.

SIDONIA THE SORCERESS, by William Meinhold, Translated by Lady Wilde, with the Amber Witch, translated by Lady Duff Gordon, in 2 vols., crown 8vo, 8s. 6d. 1894

THOMSON (James "B. V."), POETICAL WORKS, The City of Dreadful Night, Vane's Story, Weddah and Om-el-Bonain, Voice from the Hell, and Poetical Remains, Edited by B. Dobell, with Memoir and Portrait, 2 vols, thick cr. 8vo, cloth, 12s. 6d.

THOMSON (James, " B. V."), BIOGRAPHICAL AND CRITICAL STUDIES, 483 pages, cr. 8vo, cloth, 6s.

HISTORICAL, BIOGRAPHICAL WORKS, &c.

MAKERS OF MUSIC, Biographical Sketches of the Great Composers, With Chronological Summaries of their Works, and Facsimiles from Musical MSS. of Bach, Handel, Purcell, Dr. Arne, Gluck, Haydn, Mozart, Beethoven, Weber, Schubert, Berlioz, Mendelssohn, Chopin, Schumann, Wagner, Verdi, Gounod Brahms and Grieg, with General Chronological Table. By R. Farquharson Sharp, Portrait of Henry Purcell, cr. 8vo, cloth, 5s.

HOW TO MANAGE A CHORAL SOCIETY. By N. Kilburn, 2nd Edition, post 8vo., 6d.

WAGNER'S PARSIFAL and the Bayreuth Fest-Spielhaus. By N. Kilburn, cr. 8vo., 6d.

WAGNER, A Sketch of his Life and Works, by N. Kilburn, 6d.

WOMAN AS A MUSICIAN, an art Historical Study by F. R. Ritter, 8vo., 1s.

ÆSTHETICS OF MUSICAL ART, or the Beautiful in Music by Dr. F. Hand, translated by W. E. Lawson, Mus. Bac., cr. 8vo., cloth 5s.

EHLERT (LOUIS), Letters on Music to a Lady, translated by F. Raymond Ritter, cr. 8vo., bevelled cloth, gilt edges, 4s. 6d., plain cloth, 4s.

CHERUBINI, Memorials illustrative of his Life, by E. Bellasis, thick crown 8vo, cloth, 6s.

FRANZ LISZT, ARTIST AND MAN, 1811-1840, by L. Ramann, trans. by E. Cowdery, 2 vols., thick cr. 8vo, 10s. 6d. (pub. 24s.) (covers faded).

BERLIOZ, LIFE AND LETTERS, from the French by H. M. Dunstan, 2 vols., cr. 8vo., cloth, 7s. 6d. (pub. 21s.) (covers not quite fresh).

JOHANNES BRAHMS, A Biographical Sketch, translated with additions by Rosa Newmarch, edited with preface by J. A. Fuller Maitland, cr. 8vo., cl., 2s. 6d. (pub. 6s.)

THE BACH LETTERS. Letters of Samuel Wesley, relating to the Introduction into England of the Works of J. S. Bach. Edited by E. Wesley. 2nd Edition, 8vo. cloth, 2s. 6d.

CHOPIN (F.), His Life, Letters and Works, by M. Karasowski, trans. by E. Hill, *Portrait*, 2 vols, 8vo, cloth, 12s. 6d.

BALFE, His Life and Works, by W. A. Barrett, cr. 8vo, bevelled cloth, 3s. 6d. (pub. 7s. 6d.)

FREDERIC FRANCOIS CHOPIN, by Charles Willeby, with engraved portrait, cr. 8vo, cloth, 3s. 6d. (pub. 10s. 6d.)

STATHAM (H. H.), Form and Design in Music, a Brief Outline of the Æsthetic conditions of the Art, addressed to general Readers (in a readable Literary form ... in everyday language), 8vo, cloth, 2s. (pub. 5s.)

BEETHOVEN, by Richard Wagner, with a Supplement from the Philosophical Works of Arthur Schopenhauer, translated by Edward Dannreuther, Second Ed., cr. 8vo, cloth, 6s.

WAGNER, Der Ring des Nibelungen, Being the Story concisely told of Das Rhinegold, Die Walküre, Siegfried and Götterdämmerung, by N. Kilburn, post 8vo, 9d.

RICHARD WAGNER's Letters to his Dresden Friends, Theodor Uhlig, Wilhelm Fischer and Ferdinand Heine, translated with a preface by J. S. Shedlock and an etching of Wagner by O. W. Sherborn, thick cr. 8vo, cloth, gilt top, 6s. 6d. (pub. 12s. 6d.)

Box (C.), Church Music in the Metropolis, its Past and Present Condition, with Notes Critical and Explanatory, post 8vo, cloth, 3s. (covers a bit soiled).

THE PAST AND THE FUTURE, INAUGRAL LECTURE AT GRESHAM COLLEGE, Nov. 1890, by J. Frederick Bridge, Mus. Doc., cr. 8vo, sewed, 6d.

ENGLISH HYMN TUNES from the 16th Century to the Present Time, by the Rev. A. W. Malim, containing 21 Musical Illustrations, 8vo, sewed, 1s.

BEETHOVEN, Life of, by Louis Nohl, translated by John J. Lalor, 2nd Edition, cr. 8vo, bevelled cloth, gilt edges, 3s. 6d.

BEETHOVEN, Reminiscences of the artistic and Home Life of the Artist, from the diary of a Lady in close personal intercourse with him, by L. Nohl, translated by A. Wood, 8vo, cloth, 3s. 6d. (pub. 10s. 6d.)

BEETHOVEN DEPICTED BY HIS CONTEMPORARIES, by Ludwig Nohl, translated by E. Hill, 2nd Edition, thick cr. 8vo, cloth, 7s. 6d.

EDUCATIONAL.

DICTIONARY OF MUSICIANS, New and Enlarged Edition brought completely up to date, post 8vo, sewed, 1s. cloth, 1s. 6d.

MUSIC, A First Book for Beginners embodying the most recent English and Continental Teaching by a Professor [Alfred Whittingham], post 8vo, 4d.

The two principal objects kept in view in writing this little book were Thoroughness of Definition and Regular Order in the arrangement of Subjects. It differs from all other similar Works in that all the Technical Terms in Music are introduced in the Answers not in the Questions.

COUNTERPOINT: A Simple and Intelligible Treatise, Containing the most Important Rules of all Text Books, in Catechetical Form; (Forming an Answer to the Question "What is Counterpoint?") Intended for Beginners. By A. Livingstone Hirst, cr. 8vo, sewed, 9d.

MANUAL OF MUSICAL HISTORY, from the Epoch of Ancient Greece to our present time by Dr. F. L. Ritter, 2nd Edition, cr. 8vo, cl., 2s. 6d.

ON CONDUCTING, by Richard Wagner, translated by E. Dannreuther, Second Edition, cr. 8vo., cloth, 5s.

MUSIC IN AMERICA, by Dr. F. L. Ritter, cr. 8vo bevelled cloth, 7s. 6d.

DUDLEY BUCK'S Complete Pronouncing Dictionary of Musical Terms. By Dr. Dudley Buck. *New Edition with the Pronunciation of each Term accurately given,* **cr. 8vo, paper cover 6d. (cloth 1s).**

A Correct Pronouncing Dictionary of all the Terms used in Music has not yet been Published in England, though the importance of such a work for use in Schools can hardly be over estimated. A pupil going home from School with incorrect and imperfect pronunciation of Technical Terms compares unfavourably with another pupil from another school whose pronunciation is correct. The Correct Pronunciation of Musical Terms is a very simple matter, and being easily taught, and easily learned, there can be no excuse for its neglect.

THE STUDENT'S HELMHOLTZ, Musical Acoustics or the Phenomena of Sound as connected with Music, by

John Broadhouse, with more than 100 Illustrations, 3rd Edition, cr. 8vo, cloth, 7s. 6d.

THE STUDENT'S HISTORY OF MUSIC. History of Music, from the Christian Era to the present time by Dr. F. L. Ritter. 3rd Edition, thick cr. 8vo., cloth, 7s. 6d.

ELEMENTARY MUSIC. A book for Beginners, by Dr. Westbrook, with Questions and Vocal Exercises, Twelfth Edition, 1s., (cloth, 1s. 6d).

PURITY IN MUSIC, by A. F. Thibaut. Translated by J. Broadhouse. Schumann says: "A fine book about music, read it frequently." Crown 8vo., cloth, 2s. 6d.

LIFE AND WORKS OF HANDEL. By A. Whittingham. 1s. (cloth, 1s. 6d.)

LIFE AND WORKS OF MOZART. By A. Whittingham. 1s. (cloth, 1s. 6d.)

EXERCISES ON GENERAL ELEMENTARY MUSIC. A Book for Beginners, by K. Paige, 4th Edition, Part I. price 9d., Part II. price 1s. (2 parts complete in cloth, 2/4
The *Musical Times* speaks in the highest terms of this work.

DR. AHN'S FIRST FRENCH COURSE. Edited by S. Bartlett (Head Master Mercers' and Stationers' School), Post 8vo., cloth 1s. 6d.

WORKS ON THE PIANOFORTE, &c.

GREATER WORKS OF CHOPIN, (Polonaises, Mazurkas, Nocturnes, etc.) and how they should be played, by J. Kleczynski, translated by Miss N. Janotha and edited by Sutherland Edwards, with Portrait, Facsimile, etc., cr. 8vo, cloth, 5s.

MUSIC AND MUSICIANS, Essays and Criticisms, by Robert Schumann, translated, edited and annotated by F. R. Ritter, Portrait of Robert Schumann, photographed from a Crayon by Bendemann, First Series, Fourth Edition, thick cr. 8vo, cloth, 8s. 6d.

Ditto, Second Series, Second Edition, thick cr. 8vo, cloth, 10s. 6d.

EHRENFECHTER (C. A.), Technical Study in the art of Pianoforte Playing (Deppe's principles), with numerous illustrations, third edition, cr. 8vo, bevelled cloth, 2s. 6d

EHRENFECHTER (C. A.), Delivery in the Art of Pianoforte Playing, on Rhythm, Measure, Phrasing, Tempo, cr. 8vo, cloth, 2s.

BEETHOVEN'S PIANOFORTE SONATAS Explained by Ernst von Elterlein trans. by E. Hill, with Preface by Ernst Pauer, Entirely new and revised edition (the Fifth), with Portrait, Facsimile and View of House, cr. 8vo. cl., 3s. 6d.

BEETHOVEN'S SYMPHONIES in their Ideal Significance, explained by Ernst von Elterlein, translated by Francis Weber, with an account of the facts relating to Beethoven's 10th Symphony, by L. Nohl, *Second Edition*, with Portrait, cr. 8vo, cloth, 3s. 6d.

BEETHOVEN'S SYMPHONIES Critically discussed by A. T. Teetgen. *Second Edition*, cloth, 3s. 6d.

THE DEPPE FINGER EXERCISES for rapidly developing an Artistic Touch in Pianoforte playing, carefully arranged, classified and explained by Amy Fay, English Fingering, folio, 1s. 6d. (Continental Fingering, 1s. 6d.)

HOW TO PLAY CHOPIN. The Works of Chopin and their proper Interpretation. By KLECZYNSKI, translated by A. WHITTINGHAM. 3rd Ed., *Woodcut & Music Illus.* post 8vo., cloth 3s. 6d.

PLAIDY'S PIANOFORTE TEACHER'S GUIDE. Translated by F. R. RITTER. Post 8vo., boards, 1s.

SCHUMANN'S RULES AND MAXIMS for Young Musicians. 4d.

PRACTICE REGISTER for Pupils Daily Practice. A specimen, 1d., or 1s. 4d. per 100.

REEVES' VAMPING TUTOR, Art of Extemporaneous Accompaniment or Playing by Ear on the Pianoforte, rapidly enabling anyone having an ear for music (with or without any knowledge of musical notation), to accompany Waltzes, Polkas, Songs, and with equal facility in any key, with practical examples, including Ma Normandi (in C) Lilla's a Lady, The Swiss Boy, Home Sweet Home, Blue Bells of Scotland, Nancy Dawson, Ma Normandie (in A), The Miller of the Dee, by Francis Taylor, folio, 2s.

The Great Classic for the Piano.

BACH (J. S.), 48 Preludes and 48 Fugues in all the major and minor keys, in 2 vols, folio, 3s. each (or in 1 vol, stiff covers, cloth back, 7s. 6d.

MOZART'S Don Giovanni, a Commentary, from the 3rd French Edition of Charles Gounod, by W. Clark and J. T. Hutchinson, cr. 8vo, cloth, 3s. 6d.

TUNING THE PIANOFORTE.—SMITH (Hermann), The Art of Tuning the Pianoforte, a New and Comprehensive Treatise to enable the musician to Tune his Pf. upon the System founded on the Theory of Equal Temperament, cr. 8vo, limp cloth, 2s.

Readers will welcome this note of approval signed A. J. Hipkins, a name long associated with the Pianoforte, and familiar to most musicians in the musical literature of the present time. No better voucher could be desired of the fair claims of this little book upon the readers' attention and confidence "I have had the privilege of reading the proofs of Mr. Hermann Smith's clear and exhaustive treatise on Pianoforte Tuning, and I am satisfied that for the professional tuner, or the amateur who desires to understand the subject and put the knowledge he acquires into practice, there is no book upon it yet published that may be compared with it. I recommend all tuners, or would-be tuners, to study this unpretending and excellent work, wherein the theory is laid down in clear and correct terms, and the practice, as far as this is possible is indicated judiciously."

THE VIOLIN.

INFORMATION FOR PLAYERS, OWNERS, DEALERS AND MAKERS OF BOW INSTRUMENTS, ALSO FOR STRING MANUFACTURERS, taken from Personal Experiences, Studies and Observations, by William Hepworth, with Illustrations of Stainer and Guarnerius Violins, etc., cr. 8vo, cloth, 2s. 6d.

NOTICE OF ANTHONY STRADIVARI, the celebrated Violin Maker known by the name of Stradivarius, preceded by Historical and Critical Researches on the Origin and Transformations of Bow Instruments, and followed by a Theoretical Analysis of the Bow, etc., by F. J. Fetis, translated by J. Bishop, Facsimile, 8vo, cloth, 5s.

BIOGRAPHICAL DICTIONARY OF FIDDLERS, including Performers on the Violoncello and Double Bass, Past and Present, containing a Sketch of their Artistic Career, together with Notes of their Compositions, by A. Mason Clarke, with 9 portraits, post 8vo, bevelled cl., 5s.

HOW TO MAKE A VIOLIN, Practically Treated, 2 Folding Plates and many Illustrations, by J. Broadhouse, cr. 8vo, bevelled cloth, 3s. 6d.

VIOLIN MANUFACTURE IN ITALY AND ITS GERMAN ORIGIN, by Dr. E. Schebek, translated by W. E. Lawson, 8vo., sewed, 1s.

SKETCHES OF GREAT VIOLINISTS AND GREAT PIANISTS, Biographical and Anecdotal, with Account of the Violin and Early Violinists (Viotti, Spohr, Paganini, De Beriot, Ole Bull, Clementi, Moscheles, Schumann (Robert and Clara), Chopin, Thalberg, Gottschalk, Liszt), by G. T. Ferris; *Second Edition*, bevelled cloth, 3s 6d. (or gilt edges 4s. 6d.)

FACTS ABOUT FIDDLES, Violins Old and New. By J. Broadhouse, 3rd Edition, 6d.

TECHNICS OF VIOLIN PLAYING. By KARL COURVOISIER. *With Illustrations*, 4th Edition, paper 1s. (or cloth, thick paper, 2s. 6d.) Highly commended by Joachim.

HOW TO PLAY THE FIDDLE, for Beginners on the Violin. By H. W. and G. Gresswell. 4th edition, 1s.,(cl, 2s.)

AUTOBIOGRAPHY OF LOUIS SPOHR. 2 vols in 1, thick 8vo. cloth, 7s. 6d. (pub. 15s.)

TREATISE ON THE STRUCTURE AND PRESERVATION OF THE VIOLIN AND ALL OTHER BOW INSTRUMENTS, together with an account of the most celebrated makers and of the genuine characteristics of their Instruments, by J. A. Otto, with additions by J. Bishop, cr. 8vo, cloth, 3s.

WORKS ON THE ORGAN.

ANALYSIS OF MENDELSSOHN'S ORGAN WORKS, a Study of their Structural Features, for the use of Students, 127 Musical Examples, portrait and facsimiles, cr. 8vo bevelled cloth, 4s. 6d

ORGANIST'S QUARTERLY JOURNAL of Original Compositions. Edited by Dr. W. Spark, non-subscribers, 5s. net, (yearly subscriptions, 10s. 6d., post free).

New Series Volumes I and II, 160 large pages, oblong folio, bound in cloth, 18s. each.

RINK'S PRACTICAL ORGAN SCHOOL: A New Edition Carefully Revised. The Pedal Part printed on a separate Staff, and the Preface, Remarks and Technical Terms translated from the German, expressly for this edition by John Hiles. The Six Books Complete, handsomely bound in red cloth, gilt edges, ob. folio, 10s. 6d. (Issued at 20s.), or the six parts 7s. 6d. (issued at 6s. each.)

A Short History of the Organ, Organists, and Services of the Chapel of Alleyn's College, Dulwich, with Extracts from the Diary of the Founder, by W. H Stocks, cr. 8vo, sewed, 1s.

The Influence of the Organ in History. By Dudley Buck, 1s.

Henry Smart's Organ Compositions Analysed. By J. Broadhouse, cr. 8vo, cloth, 2s. 6d.

Reform in Organ Building, by Thomas Casson, 6d.

The Organ, Its Compass, Tablature, and Short and Incomplete Octaves, by John W. Warman, A.C.O. imp. 8vo, sewed, 3s. 6d. or boards, cloth back, 4s. 6d.

Catechism for the Harmonium and American Organ, by John Hiles, post 8vo, sewed, 1s.

Rimbault (Dr. E. F.), The Early English Organ Builders and their Works, from the 15th Century to the Period of the Great Rebellion, an unwritten chapter on the History of the Organ, Well printed, with woodcuts, post 8vo, cloth, 3s. 6d.

VOICE AND SINGING

Twelve Lessons on Breathing and Breath Control, for Singers, Speakers and Teachers, by Geo. E. Thorp, crown 8vo, limp cloth, 1s.

Twenty Lessons on the Development of the Voice, or Singers] Speakers and Teachers, by Geo. E. Thorp, crown 8vo, imp cloth, 1s.

50 Musical Hints to Clergymen, Management of Breath, Classification of Male Voices, Management of the Voice, The Service, with twenty specially written Exercises by Geo. F. Grover, 1s.

Catechism of Part Singing and the Choral Services. By John Hiles, 3rd Edition, thick post 8vo, price 1s.

Advice to Singers on every point of interest in reference to the Vocal Organs

THE THROAT IN ITS RELATION TO SINGING, a series of Popular Papers by Whitfield Ward, A.M., M.D. *With engravings*, cloth, 3s 6d.

HOW TO SING AN ENGLISH BALLAD. By E. Philp, 7th Edition, 6d.

VOCAL EXERCISES FOR CHOIRS AND SCHOOLS. By Dr. Westbrook, 2d.

RUDIMENTS OF VOCAL MUSIC. With 42 Preparatory Exercises, Rounds and Songs in the Treble Clef, by T. Mee Pattison, 2nd Ed., 4d.

SOME FAMOUS SONGS, an Art Historical Sketch. By F. R. Ritter. 1s.

MISCELLANEOUS.

LORD CHESTERFIELD'S LETTERS TO HIS SON.—Edited with Occasional Elucidatory Notes, Translations of all the Latin, French and Italian Quotations, and a Biographical Notice of the Author. By Chas. Stokes Carey, 2 vols, cr. 8vo, bevelled cloth, 10s. 6d.

FLAGELLATION AND THE FLAGELLANTS, A History of the Rod, in all Countries by the Rev. W. M. Cooper, *Plates and Cuts*, thick cr. 8vo, cloth, 7s. 6d. (published at 12s. 6d.)

CLASSICAL WORKS.
Edited by Prof. Anthon.

ANTHON'S HORACE, Edited by Rev. James Boyd, LL.D., thick post 8vo, 5s. 6d.

ANTHON'S HOMER'S ILIAD, First Three Books, Edited by B. Davies, LL.D., thick post 8vo, 5s 6d.

ANTHON'S CÆSAR'S COMMENTARIES, Edited by Rev. G. B. Wheeler thick post 8vo, 4s. 6d.

ANTHON'S VIRGIL, Edited by Rev. W. Trollope, M.A., thick post 8vo, 5s. 6d.

ANTHON'S ECLOGUES AND GEORGICS OF VIRGIL, with English Notes, Critical and Explanatory, and a Metrical Index, post 8vo, price 4s. 6d.

ANTHON'S SALLUST, Edited by Rev. J. Boyd, LL.D. post 8vo, 4s. 6d.

ANTHON'S JUVENAL AND PERSIUS' SATIRES, Edited by J. T. Wheeler, post 8vo, 4s. 6d.

ANTHON'S CICERO'S ORATIONS, with English Commentary and Historical, Geographical and Legal Indexes, Revised and Edited by Rev. G. B. Wheeler, post 8vo, 4s. 6d.

RUDIMENTS OF GREEK GRAMMAR, by E. Wettenhall, DD., translated by Rev. G. N. Wright, numerous annotations and Questions for Examination, by Rev. G. B. Wheeler, 3s.

NATIONAL SCHOOL OF OPERA IN ENGLAND; being The Substance of a Paper read before the Licentiates of Trinity College, March, 1882, by Frank Austin, post 8vo, sewed, 6d.

MUSICAL SHORTHAND for Composers, Students of Harmony Counterpoint, etc., can be written very rapidly and is more legible than printed music, with Specimen's from Bach, Handel, Chopin, Wagner, Mendelssohn, Spohr, Mozart, etc., by Francis Taylor, 14 pages, 12mo, 6d.

"Composers and Students of Music expend a vast amount of time in mere painful mechanism." We have only six totally unlike signs. These from their simplicity can be written with great rapidity, one dip of the pen sufficing for an entire page, and the writing being as legible as possible.—*Prefaces.*

HOW TO UNDERSTAND WAGNER'S "RING OF THE NIBELUNG," being the Story and a Descriptive Analysis of the "Rheingold," the "Valkyr," "Siegfried" and the "Dusk of the Gods," with a number of Musical Examples by Gustave Kobbé, Sixth Edition, post 8vo, cloth, 3s. 6d.

"To be appreciated in the smallest way Wagner must be studied in advance.—*Illustrated London News.*

RATIONAL ACCOMPANIMENT TO THE PSALMS by F. Gilber Webb, post 8vo, 6d.

HOW TO PLAY FROM SCORE.—Treatise on Accompaniment from Score on the Organ or Pianoforte, by

F. J. Fetis, trans. by A. Whittingham, cr. 8vo, cloth, 3s. 6d.

FRANZ LISZT, by T. Carlaw Martin, 6d. (No. 10 St. Cecilia Biography Series).

LIFE OF ROBERT SCHUMANN, with Letters, 1833-1852, by von Wasielewski, Translated by A. L. Alger, with Preface by W. A. Barrett, B. Mus. cr. 8vo, cloth, 8s. 6d.

VOICE PRODUCTION AND VOWEL ENUNCIATION, by F. F. Mewburn Levien, Diagrams by Arthur C. Behrend, post 8vo, 6d.

"The most informing and interesting of all the Musical Journals."

THE MUSIC STUDENT.—A Scholastic Musica Monthly for Professor and Pupil, Devoted to the Violin Pianoforte, Singing, Harmony and Composition, Monthly 2d. (by post 2½d.), Annual Subscription, post free, 2s. 6d. (Abroad post free, 3s.)

CHOIR LISTS FOR SUNDAY SERVICES.

No. 1. Morning and Evening, printed in red, 1s. 4d. per 100.

No. 2. Morning, Afternoon, and Evening, printed in red, 1s. 6d. per 100.

No. 3. Morning and Evening, printed in red and black, 1s. 8d. per 100.

No. 4. Morning and Even., printed in red 1s. 4d. per 100.

No. 5. Quarto Size, Matins, Litany, Holy Communion, First Evensong, Second Evensong, Gothic Letter, printed in red, 6d. per dozen, 3s. per 100.

CHOIR ATTENDANCE REGISTER, 8vo, cloth.

No. 1. Ruled for a Choir of 20 or less, for one year, beginning at any date, 1s. 6d.

No. 2. Ruled for a Choir of 40 or less, for one year, beginning at any date, 2s.

No. 3. Ruled for a choir of 60 or less, for one year, beginning at any date, 2s. 6d.

NATIONAL AND PATRIOTIC SONG ALBUM, with Pf. Acc., containing the following popular pieces:—
A handsome Copyright Folio Volume of 81 pages, with coloured cover, printed on good paper, 2s. 6d.

(Formerly R. Cocks & Co.)

God Bless the Prince of Wales
Dear England
Victoria
God Bless our Sailor Prince
Here's a Health unto His Majesty
Lord of the Sea
The Roast Beef of Old England
The Blue Bells of Scotland
Tom Bowling
Come Lassies and Lads
Ye Mariners of England
The Bay of Biscay
Hearts of Oak
Stand United
The Cause of England's Greatness
The Last Rose of Summer
The Leather Bottle
Home Sweet Home
Three Cheers for the Red White and Blue
The Minstrel Boy
The British Grenadiers
Auld Lang Syne
Rule Britannia
God Save the Queen
Short Biographical Sketches

MODERN CHURCH MUSIC.

1. Easter Anthem, "Jesus Lives!" by Rev. T. Herbert Spinney, price 2d.
2. Anthem for Whitsuntide and General Use, "Come Holy Ghost our Souls Inspire," by Thomas Adams, F.R.C.O., price 2d.
3. Story of the Ascension, by Rev. John Napleton, price 1½d.
4. Anthem, "God so Loved the World," by J. Jamouneau, price 2d.
5. Magnificat in B flat, by Thomas Adams, F.R.C.O., Price 3d.
6. Nunc Dimittis in B flat, by Thomas Adams, F.R.C.O., Price 2d.
7. Four Kyries, by Charles Steggall, Berthold Tours, E. J. Hopkins, J. M. W. Young, price 1½d.
8. Te Deum, by T. E. Spinney, 1½d.
9. Anthem, "I am the Good Shepherd," by G. Rayleigh Vicars, 2d.
10. Story of the Cross, Music by H. Clifton Bowker, 2d.

POPULAR PART SONGS.
1. Merrily goes the Mill, by T. B. Southgate, 1d.
2. Take, O Take those Lips away, Part Song for S.A.T.B. by Claude E. Cover, A.R.C.O., 1½d.
3. Pack Clouds Away, for S.A.T.B.; by Claude E. Cover, A.R.C.O., 2d.

MARCHES, for the Pianoforte by John Philip Sousa, Folio Album, 1s., containing:—
1. The Washington Post.
2. Manhatton Beach.
3. The Liberty Bell.
4. High School Cadets.
5. The Belle of Chicago.
6. The Corcoran Cadets.
7. Our Flirtation.
8. March past of the Rifle Regiment.
9. March past of the National Fencibles.
10. Semper Fidelis.

Performing Edition.

THE CREATION, A Sacred Oratorio composed by Joseph Haydn, Vocal Score, The Pianoforte Accompaniment arranged and the whole edited by G. A. Macfarren, 8vo, paper covers, 2s., boards, 2s. 6d., scarlet cloth, 4s.

SIXTY YEARS OF MUSIC: A Record of the Art in England during the Victorian Era, containing 70 Portraits of the most Eminent Musicians, oblong quarto, boards, cloth back, 2s. 6d.

THE ORGANIST'S QUARTERLY JOURNAL
Of Original Compositions.

Founded by DR. Wm. SPARK, Late Organist, Town Hall, Leeds

Non-subscribers, 5/- each. Subscription, 10/6 for 4 issues.

Series, Vol 1, containing 160 large pages, bound in cloth, 18s.

Part 12. New Series
1. IN MEMORIAM - - - - Rev. GEOF. C. RYLY, M.A., Mus. Bac., Oxon.
2. TOCCATA - - - - - G. B. POLLERI.
3. OVERTURE from Epiphany ALFRED KING, M.D.

Part 11, New Series.
1. PRELUDE AND FUGUE with POSTLUDE E. A. CHAMBERLAYNE.
2. PRELUDE AND FUGUE - - - F. YOUNG.
3. FUGUE - - - - ARCHIBALD DONALD.
4. FUGUE - - - - WILLIAM HOPE.

Part 10, New Series.
1. FUGUE - - - - ARCHIBALD DONALD.
2. PRELUDE AND FUGUE with POSTLUDE E. A. CHAMBERLAYNE.
3. PRELUDE AND FUGUE - - - F. YOUNG.
 - - - - SIR G. ELVEY.

Part 9, New Series.
1. ANDANTE CON MOTO - - W. A MONTGOMERY, L.T.C.L.
2. FANTASIA in E minor CUTHBERT HARRIS, Mus. B.,
3. POSTLUDE at Ephes. V. v. 19.
   Si tibi placeat, Mihi con displicet
   W. CONRADI, (Y. of B. 1816).
   Org. St. Paul's Church, Schwerin i/m Germany,
4. HARVEST MARCH - - - HENRY J. POOLE.

Part 8, New Series.
1. SCHERZO MINUET - - W. MULLINEUX,
   Organist of the Town Hall, Bolton.
2. INTRODUCTION to the Hymn on the Passion,
   O Haupt Voll Blut und Wunden" - W. CONRADI,
   Organist Paul's Church, Schwerin, Germany,
3. THESIS AND ANTITHESIS, or DISPUTE, APPEASEMENT, CONCILIATION - - - W. CONRADI,
   Organist Paul's Church, Schwerin, Germany.
4. CARILLON in E - - - CUTHBERT HARRIS, Mus. B., F.R.C.O., &c.
5. ANDANTE "Hope" - - - INGLIS BERVON.
6. ORCHESTRAL MARCH in C - JAMES CRAPPER.
   L. Mus., Organist of the Parish Ch., Kirkcudbright.

Part 7, New Series.
1. ANDANTE GRAZIOSO in G
   CHAS. B. MELVILLE, F.R.C.O.
2. POLISH SONG - - - - - CHOPIN.
   Arranged for the organ by PERCIVAL GARRETT.
3. INTRODUCTION, VARIATIONS, and FINALE on the
   Hymn Tune "Rockingham" CH. R. FISHER, Mus. B.
4. TWO SOFT MOVEMENTS - W. C. FILEY, I.S.M.
   1. "Espérance." 2. "Tendresse."
5. ANDANTE in A flat - - W. GRIFFIN, Mus. B.
   Org. of St. Sepulchre Church, Northampton.
6. FUGUE, 4 Voice, 3 Subjects - DR. J. C. TILEY.

The Organist's Quarterly Journal (cont.).

Part 6, New Series.
CON MOTO MODERATO in C
    ORLANDO A. MANSFIELD, MUS.B., F.R.C.O.
2. TEMPO DI MENUETTO - - - GEO. H. ELY.
3. DIRGE IN MEMORIAM, REGINALD ADKINS
    J. E. ADKINS, F.R.C.O.
4. ANDANTE in F - - - - R. H. HEATH.
5. ABERYSTWYTH OFFERTOIRE - J. G. MOUNTFORD.
6. ANDANTE in D (Prière) - E. EVELYN BARRON, M.A.

Part 5, New Series.
1. ALLEGRETTO SCHERZANDO in A flat W.E.ASHMALL.
2. ANDANTE RELIGIOSO in G - DR. J. BRADFORD.
3. MARCH POMPOSO in E flat - CHARLES DARNTON.
4. ANDANTE CON MOTO "Twilight"
    CH. R. FISHER, MUS. B.
5. MINUET in F - - W E. BELCHER, F.R.C.O

Part 4, New Series.
1. ANDANTE MODERATO - - - F. READ.
2. PRELUDE AND FUGUE in D minor
    E. A. CHAMBERLAYNE.
3. SKETCH - - - ARTHUR GEO. COLBORN.
4. FUGUE - - - - JAMES TURPIN.
5. ALLEGRO - - CHARLES H. FISHER.
6. MARCHE MYSTIQUE - THEME BY ROLAND
    DE LASSUS.—A Relic of Ancient Times.

Part 3, New Series.
1. MINUET AND TRIO in F.
    ED. J. BELLERBY, MUS. B., OXON.
2. "DUNDEE" ("or French") - JOHN P. ATTWATER.
3. ADAGIO. An Elegy, in G minor
    CHAS. R. FISHER, MUS. B.
4. ANDANTE, A major - - E. F. HORNER
5. ALLEGRO, D minor - - GEO. MINNS (Ely

Part 2, New Series.
1. TOCCATA FANTASIA (Study in C minor)
    E. T. DRIFFIELD.
2. ANDANTE GRAZIOSO - - - W. FAULKES.
3. MARCHE FUNEBRE ARTHUR WANDERER.
4. ANDANTE SEMPLICE E. A. CHAMBERLAYNE.
5. FESTAL MARCH - - A. W. KETELBEY.

Part 1, New Series.
1. OFFERTOIRE in A minor - FRED. W. DAL (Leipzig).
2. SECOND FANTASIA on SCOTCH AIRS
    WILLIAM SPARK.
3. ADESTE FIDELES with Variations and Fugue)
    CHARLES HUNT.
4. INTERMEZZO - G. TOWNSEND DRIFFIELD.

Part 103, July 1894.
1. POSTLUDE in G FREDERICK W. HOLLOWAY, F.C.O
2. SUITE: No. 1, PRELUDE; No. 2, BERCEUSE;
    No. 3, TOCCATA - LAURENT PARODI (Genoa
3. NOCTURNE - - - - WILLIAM LOCKETT.
4. ANDANTE PASTORALE in B minor
    JACOB BRADFORD, MUS. D., OXON
5. INTRODUCTORY VOLUNTARY - ALBERT W. KETELBEY
6. FUGUE - - - - R. J. ROWE, L.R.A.M.

LONDON: WILLIAM REEVES, 83, CHARING CROSS ROAD, W.C.

BOOKS ON FREEMASONRY

PUBLISHED BY

WM. REEVES, 83, Charing Cross Road, W.C.

12mo, red cloth, gilt, 323 pp., 3/6
Carlile (R.), Manual of Freemasonry, containing the First Three Degrees, The Royal Arch and Knights' Templar Druids, The Degrees of Mark Man, Mark Master, Architect, Grand Architect., etc., etc.

12mo, blue cloth, gilt, 374 pp., 3/6
Fellows (J.), Mysteries of Freemasonry; or, An Exposition of the Religious Dogmas and Customs of the Ancient Egyptians; showing, from the origin, nature and objects of the rites and ceremonies of remote antiquity, their identity with the Order of Modern Masonry, with some remarks on the Metamorphosis of Apuleius, *with numerous illustrative woodcuts.*

12mo, green cloth, gilt, 254 pp., 3/6
Ritual and Illustrations of Freemasonry, *accompanied by very numerous engravings,* and a Key to the Phi Beta Kappa.

8vo, sewed, 26 pp. 1/-
Investigation into the Cause of the Hostility of the Church of Rome to Freemasonry, and an Inquiry into Freemasonry as it Was, and Is: with a Criticism as to how far the Order fulfils its Functions, by the Author of "The Text Book of Freemasonry."

Post 8vo, sewed, 48 pp., 1/-
Joachin and Boaz; or, an Authentic Key to the Door of Freemasonry, both Ancient and Modern.

Post 8vo sewed, 50 pp., 1/-
Three Distinct Knocks at the Door of the Most Ancient Freemasonry.

8vo, sewed, 1/-
The Origin of Freemasonry, or the 1717 Theory Exploded, by C. J. Paton, 8vo. 1s.

8vo, paper, 2/6 (post free 3/-)
Weisse (John A.), The Obelisk of Freemasonry, according to the Discoveries of Belzoni and Commander Gorringe: also Egyptian Symbols compared with those discovered in American Mounds.

Fifth thousand, 12mo, cloth 1/-
Pocket Lexicon of Freemasonry, by W. J. Morris, 18° P.D.D.G.M., St. Lawrence, District and Past Inspector Gen. Royal and Select Masters.

12mo, cloth, 62 pp., 2/-
Fox (T. L.), Freemasonry; An Account of the Early History of Freemasonry in England, with Illustrations of the Principles and Precepts advocated by that Institution.

Any of the above sent POST FREE *upon receipt of Remittance for price named.*

BOOKS ON FREEMASONRY

PUBLISHED BY
WM. REEVES, 83, Charing Cross Road, W.C.

12mo, blue cloth, red edges, 5/- (or calf limp, gilt edges, 10/6.)

Text Book of Freemasonry; a Complete Handbook of Instruction to all the Workings in the Various Mysteries and Ceremonies of CRAFT MASONRY, containing the Entered Apprentice, Fellow-craft, and Master Mason's degrees; the Ceremony of Installation of the W. Master and Officers of the Lodge, together with the whole of the Three Lectures; also the Ceremony of Exhaltation in the Supreme Order of the Holy Royal Arch, a Selection of Masonic Songs, etc., *illustrated with four engravings of the* **TRACING BOARDS**, by "A Member of the Craft," new and revised edition.

Ditto, Ditto, on thin paper, bound in leather pocket-book style, 5s.

The Three Tracing Boards, in 12mo, cloth line, 1s. 6d.

Ditto, Larger Size, roy. 8vo, 4 plates, 1s. 6d.

Post 8vo, cloth, 278 pp., 10/- (or crimson calf limp. gilt edges, 15/-

Text Book of Advanced Freemasonry, containing for the self-instruction of Candidates, the COMPLETE RITUALS of the HIGHER DEGREES, viz., Royal Ark Mariners, Mark Master, Royal Arch, Red Cross of Rome and Constantinople, Knights' Templar and Rose Croix de Heredom; also Monitorial Instructions on the 30th to the 33rd and last degree of Freemasonry, to which are added Historical Introductions and Explanatory remarks by the Author of the "Text Book."

8vo, cloth, 300 pp., 3/6

HONE (William), Ancient Mysteries described, especially the English Miracle Plays founded on the Apocryphal New Testament Story, extant among the unpublished MSS. in the British Museum, including notices of Ecclesiastical shows and Festivals of Fools and Asses, the English Boy Bishop Descent into Hell, the Lord Mayor's Show, the Guildhall Giants, Christmas Carols, etc., with engravings and Index.

8vo, cloth, 3/6

HONE (William) The Apocryphal New Testament, being all the Gospels, Epistles and other pieces now extant attributed in the first four centuries to Jesus Christ, his Apostles and their Companions and not included in the New Testament by its compilers.

Any of the above sent POST FREE *upon receipt of Remittance for price named.*

THE o:—— Weekly One Penny (or f with Supplement 2d
(One week after date always 2d).

"MUSICAL STANDARD,"

A NEWSPAPER FOR MUSICIANS, - - - -
PROFESSIONAL AND AMATEUR.

Gives Supplements of Illustrations of British and Foreign Organs, Portraits of Eminent Musicians, Organ Music, Violin Music, Anthems, Part Songs, etc.

Yearly subscription 7s. 6d., abroad, 9s. 9d., post free.

Illustrated Series, Vols. 1, 2, 3, 4, 5, 6, 7, 8, 9 & 10 bound in brown cloth, 5s. each.

Handsome Covers for Binding, 1s. 6d. each, (by post 1s. 9d).

Publishing and Advertising Offices:
83, CHARING CROSS ROAD, LONDON, W.C.

Paper, 2s.: or Cloth, 3s. 6d.

MUSICAL DIRECTORY

FOR GREAT BRITAIN AND IRELAND.

THE TRADES, PROFESSORS AND OTHERS CONNECTED WITH MUSIC, CHORAL SOCIETIES, STAFF OF CATHEDRALS, COLLEGES AND ABBEY CHURCHES, ETC.

W. REEVES, 83, CHARING CROSS ROAD, LONDON, W.C.

THE ORGANIST'S QUARTERLY JOURNAL

Of Original Compositions.

FOUNDED BY DR. WILLIAM SPARK
City Organist, Leeds.

New Series VOLUMES I. & II., *containing 160 large pages bound in cloth, 18s. each.*

For list of the Contents of the Parts. See pages 16 & 17

W. REEVES, 83, CHARING CROSS ROAD, W.C.

The Violin Times,

Monthly, 2d.,
(by post 2½d.)

Edited by E. POLONASKI.

Subscription, 2s. 6d., per Year, - Abroad, 3s.
VOLS. 1 TO 5, BOUND, PRICE 6/- EACH. Covers for binding 2s. each.

JUST READY. 8vo. boards, cloth back, 6/- net.

The International
DIRECTORY OF PATENT AGENTS.
New and Enlarged Edition (*the third*) 1901,
Contains over 4000 Patent Agents, practising in all parts of the world. Arranged Alphabetically and also Geographically.

London : **W. Reeves, 83, Charing Cross Road, W.C.**

The most Informing and Interesting of all the Musical Journals

THE . . . Monthly 2d Post Free 2½d
MUSIC STUDENT,
A Scholastic Musical Monthly for Professor and Pupil,
ESPECIALLY DEVOTED TO
THE VIOLIN, PIANO, SINGING, HARMONY AND COMPOSITION.
Annual Subscription 2s. 6d.   Abroad 3s.

LEADING FEATURES.

ARTICLES BY EXPERTS on Pianoforte, Violin and Mandoline Playing, Singing, Harmony, Acoustics, &c.

GREAT COMPOSERS, their Music and its Character.

ENGLAND'S MUSIC TEACHERS. Notices, with portraits of Teachers in all parts of the Kingdom.

AIDS AND HELPS FOR BUSY TEACHERS AND EARNEST STUDENTS.

ANALYSIS OF PIECES set for the principal Violin and Pianoforte Exams.; Advice to Candidates; Hints of Paper Work, &c.

OUR HARMONY CLASS. A practical course of Harmony training.

HOME ORCHESTRAS AND MUSICAL CLUBS.

REPLIES TO QUERIES.

"PRO AND CON." Our Readers' views on subjects of musical interest.

NOTICES OF NEW MUSIC.

THE CONCERT GIVER. Brief accounts of Concerts given in London and the Provinces.

NOTES AND JOTTINGS OF THE MONTH;
ANECDOTES OF MUSICIANS
ACADEMICAL SUCCESSES, &c.

All communications respecting this Journal should be addressed to the Publisher :—

WILLIAM REEVES, 83, Charing Cross Road, London, W.C

www.ingramcontent.com/pod-product-compliance
Lightning Source LLC
Chambersburg PA
CBHW022016220426
43663CB00007B/1096